ETHNOGRAPHY
Second Edition

Applied Social Research Methods Series
Volume 17

APPLIED SOCIAL RESEARCH METHODS SERIES

Series Editors
LEONARD BICKMAN, Peabody College, Vanderbilt University, Nashville
DEBRA J. ROG, Vanderbilt University, Washington, DC

Other volumes in this series are listed at the back of the book

ETHNOGRAPHY
Second Edition

Step by Step

David M. Fetterman

Applied Social Research Methods Series
Volume 17

SAGE Publications
International Educational and Professional Publisher
Thousand Oaks   London   New Delhi

For information:

SAGE Publications, Inc.
2455 Teller Road
Thousand Oaks, California 91320
E-mail: order@sagepub.com

SAGE Publications Ltd.
6 Bonhill Street
London EC2A 4PU
United Kingdom

SAGE Publications India Pvt. Ltd.
M-32 Market
Greater Kailash I
New Delhi 110 048 India

Printed in the United States of America

Library of Congress Cataloging-in-Publication Data

Fetterman, David M.
    Ethnography: Step by step / by David M. Fetterman.—2nd ed.
        p. cm.—(Applied social research methods ; v. 17)
    Includes bibliographical references and index.
    ISBN 0-7619-1384-X (alk. paper). — ISBN 0-7619-1385-8 (pbk.: alk. paper)
    1. Ethnology—Methodology. I. Title. II. Series: Applied social research
methods series ; v. 17.
GN345.F47 1998
305.8'001—dc21   97-33800

99   00   01   02   03   10   9   8   7   6   5   4   3

Acquiring Editor:	C. Deborah Laughton
Editorial Assistant:	Eileen Carr
Production Editor:	Astrid Virding
Production Assistant:	Karen Wiley
Typesetter/Designer:	Marion S. Warren
Print Buyer:	Anna Chin

Contents

I like to walk amidst the beautiful things that adorn the world.

—George Santayana

Preface

As a practicing anthropologist, I apply anthropological concepts to real-world problems on a daily basis. This applied background influences my discussion of ethnography from the first step to the last. This bias has helped me to delimit the vast topic of ethnography to a few bare essentials. Ethnography is more than a 1-day hike through the woods. It is an ambitious journey through the complex world of social interaction.

This book represents one of many paths on this journey. Its purpose is to enable other researchers to enjoy their journeys and to reach their destinations. This is not a simple how-to book. It is a companion volume for the practicing ethnographer. Like a travelog, it identifies and discusses the major landmarks every ethnographer and potential ethnographer encounters. Ironically, reaching a destination in ethnography often means taking false paths, coming up against dead ends or detours, and sometimes losing the way altogether. I hope that this book will be a useful guide for the initiate, a valuable tool for the teacher, and an enjoyable refresher for the experienced ethnographer.

This edition takes a step into a new frontier—the Internet. The Internet is one of the most powerful resources available to ethnographers. This edition provides insight into the uses of the Internet, including conducting searches about topics or sites, collecting census data, conducting interviews by "chatting" and videoconferencing, sharing notes and pictures about research sites, debating issues with colleagues on listservs and in on-line journals, and downloading useful data collection and analysis software. These tools are rapidly becoming indispensable to ethnographers today.

Acknowledgments

I am indebted to many friends. The students, program participants, natives, administrators, sponsors, and colleagues I have worked with in a multitude of studies and in hundreds of settings all over the world have helped shape my understanding of what ethnography is all about. Their experience has contributed greatly to this book.

I also owe a debt of gratitude to those who contributed to my intellectual development, specifically in educational and medical anthropology. I must single out George and Louise Spindler and Bert Pelto, who helped to lay the foundation of my ethnographic understanding.

Psychometric assistance in many of the studies discussed in this text was provided by G. Kasten Tallmadge, Lee J. Cronbach, and Ed Haertel. These colleagues, along with Lee Shulman, Joseph Greenberg, Jim Gibbs, Lois-ellin Datta, and many other friends and colleagues from the Council on Anthropology and Education, the American Evaluation Association, the Society for Applied Anthropology, and the American Educational Research Association helped to refine my understanding of ethical and policy decision making.

Harry Wolcott, Michael Patton, Debra Rog, and Elaine Simon generously provided their comments and suggestions during various stages of the development of this book. Their ideas were on target and useful.

Gene Glass became a good friend and provided a critical eye conceptually and editorially during the process of completing this second edition. He is a colleague who understands the power and promise of research, including ethnography, on the Internet and his insights and assistance in this area are hard to match.

Thanks are also due to two additional friends, C. Deborah Laughton and Leonard Bickman, for providing the necessary support and flexibility for me to complete this new edition.

Deborah S. Waxman, a lifelong companion, has provided invaluable assistance, helping me navigate through many of the studies discussed in this book. She has also greatly assisted me in organizing and editing the manuscript.

Sarah Rachel, my daughter, deserves thanks for reminding us of the simple joys of inquiry, exploration, and understanding.

1

The First Step: An Overview

*A journey of a thousand miles
must begin with a single step.*

—Lao-tzu

Ethnography is the art and science of describing a group or culture. The description may be of a small tribal group in an exotic land or a classroom in middle-class suburbia. The task is much like the one taken on by an investigative reporter, who interviews relevant people, reviews records, weighs the credibility of one person's opinions against another's, looks for ties to special interests and organizations, and writes the story for a concerned public and for professional colleagues. A key difference between the investigative reporter and the ethnographer, however, is that whereas the journalist seeks out the unusual—the murder, the plane crash, or the bank robbery—the ethnographer writes about the routine, daily lives of people. The more predictable patterns of human thought and behavior are the focus of inquiry.

Ethnographers are noted for their ability to keep an open mind about the group or culture they are studying. This quality, however, does not imply any lack of rigor. The ethnographer enters the field with an open mind, not an empty head. Before asking the first question in the field, the ethnographer begins with a problem, a theory or model, a research design, specific data collection techniques, tools for analysis, and a specific writing style.

The ethnographer also begins with biases and preconceived notions about how people behave and what they think—as do researchers in every field. Indeed, the choice of what problem, geographic area, or people to study is in itself biased. Biases serve both positive and negative functions. When controlled, biases can focus and limit the research effort. When uncontrolled, they can undermine the quality of ethnographic research. To mitigate the negative effects of bias, the ethnographer must first make specific biases explicit. A series of additional quality controls, such as

1

triangulation, contextualization, and a nonjudgmental orientation, place a check on the negative influence of bias. An open mind also allows the ethnographer to explore rich, untapped sources of data not mapped out in the research design. The ethnographic study allows multiple interpretations of reality and alternative interpretations of data throughout the study. The ethnographer is interested in understanding and describing a social and cultural scene from the emic, or insider's, perspective. The ethnographer is both storyteller and scientist; the closer the reader of an ethnography comes to understanding the native's point of view, the better the story and the better the science.

This chapter presents an overview of the steps involved in ethnographic work. The following chapters elaborate these steps in detail. The process begins when the ethnographer selects a problem or topic and a theory or model to guide the study. The ethnographer simultaneously chooses whether to follow a basic or applied research approach to delineate and shape the effort. The research design then provides a basic set of instructions about what to do and where to go during the study. Fieldwork is the heart of the ethnographic research design. In the field, basic anthropological concepts, data collection methods and techniques, and analysis are the fundamental elements of "doing ethnography." Selection and use of various pieces of equipment—including the human instrument—facilitate the work. This process becomes product through analysis at various stages in ethnographic work—in field notes, memoranda, interim reports, and, most dramatically, the published report, article, or book.

The following chapters present these steps in a logical order, using concrete case examples throughout to illustrate each step. This step-by-step approach also highlights the utility of planning and organization in ethnographic work. The more organized the ethnographer, the easier is his or her task of making sense of the mountains of data collected in the field. Sifting through notepads filled with illegible scrawl, listening to hours of tape recordings, labeling and organizing piles of pictures and slides, and cross-referencing disks of data are much less threatening to the ethnographer who has taken an organized, carefully planned approach.

The reality, however, is that ethnographic work is not always orderly. It involves serendipity, creativity, being in the right place at the right or wrong time, much hard work, and old-fashioned luck. Thus, although this text proceeds within the confines of an orderly structure, I have made a concerted effort to ensure that it also conveys the unplanned, sometimes chaotic, and always intriguing character of ethnographic research.

Whereas in most research, analysis follows data collection, in ethnographic research analysis and data collection begin simultaneously. An ethnographer is a human instrument and must discriminate among different types of data and analyze the relative worth of one path over another at every turn in fieldwork, well before any formalized analysis takes place. Clearly, ethnographic research involves many different levels of analysis. Analysis is an ongoing responsibility and joy from the first moment an ethnographer envisions a new project to the final stages of writing and reporting the findings.

THE PROBLEM

Ethnographic research begins with the selection of a problem or topic of interest. The research problem that the ethnographer chooses guides the entire research endeavor. It typically dictates the shape of the research design, including the budget, the tools to conduct the research, and even the presentation of the research findings. How the ethnographer interprets and defines the problem usually reflects either a basic or an applied research orientation. The problem may also suggest the most appropriate research approach—ethnographic, survey, or experimental.

A researcher can address a problem—such as unequal minority representation in higher-paying and higher-status occupations in the United States—in many ways. For example, a survey approach would probably be more efficient than an ethnographic approach in determining the number of ethnic groups in specific occupations throughout the United States. A descriptive approach such as ethnography, however, would be most useful to study how unequal representation in specific occupations comes about, including how cultural values are transmitted to create institutional racism and what people think about this inequity. To determine the impact of programs to ameliorate economic differences between specific ethnic groups, a quasi-experimental design accompanied by a descriptive approach would be most appropriate. Research problem definition, therefore, is really a statement about what the ethnographer wants to know.

In essence, the problem or its definition is the driving force behind the research endeavor. The problem must precede the selection of a research method to avoid the trap of having a method in search of a problem—a situation that produces frustrating and imprecise results.

BASIC OR APPLIED ROLE

The researcher's role further refines the definition of the problem. A study of the incest taboo appears to be classic anthropological or psychological research. More specific questions are necessary, however, before the researcher can determine the appropriate classification: basic or applied; anthropological, psychological, or sociological; and so on. In this instance, the issue most relevant to proper classification is a function of the type of questions posed.

An ethnographic study of incest raises questions of social organization and cultural rules and regulations. Arthur Wolf's (1970) ethnographic study of incest in China is a classic example of basic research. His work supports Westermarck's hypothesis that intimate childhood contact promotes sexual aversion rather than Freud's contention that the taboo is imposed to prohibit incestuous behavior. This work is primarily theoretical in nature, without any policy, pragmatic, or timely application.

A study of incest can also be an applied ethnographic task. Phelan's (1987) work in this area is a good example. Phelan studied what incest means in U.S. society. She found significant differences between the behavior and perceptions of incestuous natural fathers and those of stepfathers. For example, natural fathers were more likely to have intercourse with their children because they considered them extensions of themselves. Her work raised important questions about the role of the incest taboo, and her research had direct implications for treatment facilities throughout the country. Wolf's (1970) basic research approach to the problem of incest involved long-term fieldwork and years of sifting through familial and government records. Phelan's applied research approach required less time in the field and less time sifting through records. Whereas Phelan's applied research had significant implications for immediate practical counseling approaches, with some less powerful theoretical impact, Wolf's research findings had significant implications for kinship theory, with little or no immediate practical significance. Basic research is conceptualized and designed by the researcher, who seeks funding—typically a grant—from a potentially interested sponsor. The findings are reported in refereed journals. The applied research effort, often funded by a contract, is a fully developed response to a sponsor's expressed interest in the topic. Its findings are published in reports for the sponsor.

Despite these differences, the boundaries between basic and applied research become fuzzier every day. Many applied researchers now have an established research interest with significant theoretical implications, and they search for a sponsor with stated similar interests in a request for proposals. Furthermore, they are publishing more frequently in refereed journals and scholarly texts—not unlike basic researchers, who have career interests and seek funding from interested sponsors. The traditional differences that characterize each type of researcher, however, still hold, and these also characterize the relationship between the problem and how it is articulated, researched, and written about.

THEORY

Theory is a guide to practice; no study, ethnographic or otherwise, can be conducted without an underlying theory or model. Whether it is an explicit anthropological theory or an implicit personal model about how things work, the researcher's theoretical approach helps define the problem and how to tackle it.

When my father taught me how to fix a leaky faucet, he began by explaining the first law of thermodynamics and hydraulic theory before showing me how to stop the leak. Although he was clearly more interested in theory than in practice, because of that lesson I have never forgotten to shut off the water before working on the plumbing. His philosophical approach also helped me to understand how all the pieces worked together. In essence, he provided a theoretical road map, explaining the theories by demonstrating how each piece of the fixture worked.

Everyone tackles a problem with a theory or set of theories in mind about how things work. The trick is to select the most appropriate level of theory for the task at hand. I argue, for instance, that a simple flowchart would have told me how to fix the faucet just as easily (and in much less time) than my father's highly technical, explicitly theoretical approach.

The ethnographer recognizes the importance of understanding the epistemological basis for a selected model. The typical model for ethnographic research is based on a phenomenologically oriented paradigm. This paradigm embraces a multicultural perspective because it accepts multiple realities. People act on their individual perceptions, and those actions have real consequences—thus the subjective reality each individual sees is no less real than an objectively defined and measured reality. Phenomenologically oriented studies are generally inductive; they make few explicit assumptions about sets of relationships. Such an approach is the basis of grounded theory (Glaser & Strauss, 1967): The theory underlying a sociocultural system or community develops directly from empirical data.

A positivistic paradigm stands in stark contrast to phenomenology. Unlike the typical ethnographer, an experimental psychologist is more likely to adopt a positivistic paradigm. Positivism assumes the existence of an objective reality, is typically deductive in approach, and establishes a priori assumptions about relationships.

The ethnographer has a vast array of specific theories from which to choose. Each theory has application for specific topics and is uninformative or misleading when applied to inappropriate problems. Theories that offer little explanatory power, are inappropriate for most topics, or have been debunked are best left rotting on the vine. Most researchers, explicitly or implicitly, use one of two types of theory: ideational or materialistic. Ideational theories suggest that fundamental change is the result of mental activity—thoughts and ideas. Materialists believe that material conditions—ecological resources, money, and modes of production—are the prime movers. Neither approach answers all problems; individual ethnographers select one of the two approaches to suit their training, personality, and specific needs or questions of interest.

Cognitive theory is the most popular ideational theory in anthropology today. Cognitive theory assumes that we can describe what people think by listening to what they say—not an unreasonable assumption. Using linguistically driven (ethnosemantic) techniques, we can create taxonomies of how people view the world. For example, we may learn from Eskimos about their conception of snow—specifically, that they identify many types of snow within the larger category, corresponding to its many uses in their lives. Ideational theory researchers view the human world from the perspective of its mental origins—ideas, cognitive maps, beliefs, and knowledge. Classic ideational theories in anthropology include culture and personality theory (including psychoanalytic theory), sociolinguistics (Cazden, 1979; Gumperz, 1972; Heath, 1982), symbolic interactionism (Blumer, 1969), and ethnomethodology (Bogdan & Taylor, 1975; Garfinkel, 1967; Mehan, 1987; Mehan & Wood, 1975).

In contrast, ethnographers who adopt materialist theories view the world according to observable behavior patterns. A limited but classic political and economic materialist theory is historical materialism, or neo-Marxism. Marxist theory assumes that all change results from shifts in the modes of production and in the control over these modes. Economic forces, class consciousness, class conflict, and various forms of social organization drive social and cultural change. Other materialist approaches in anthropology include technoenvironmentalism (Harris, 1971) and cultural ecology (Geertz, 1963; Steward, 1955).

I found many theories useful in my study of a national program for dropouts—the Career Intern Program (CIP). Both static and dynamic theories were necessary to understand what was going on. A static functionalist theory (Geertz, 1957; Radcliffe-Brown, 1952; Vogt, 1960), combined with the static equilibrium model (Gluckman, 1968), was useful in creating a descriptive baseline. A structural functionalist approach made the structure and function of the schools and their relationship to the various government and quasi-government institutions easy to map. The equilibrium model allowed me to hold everything still, as if the situation were in stasis for a moment, to identify where everyone stood in the picture. The theory and the model used were useful in establishing a baseline to begin observations of change over time. These approaches, however, are generally regarded as static—not sufficient for the study of sociocultural change.[1]

One dynamic theory that guided the study of the CIP for dropouts was innovation theory (Barnett, 1953). The experimental program for dropouts was the innovation in question. This theory helped me pigeonhole observations about the innovative program, ranging from its introduction through the intricate maze to its acceptance, rejection, modification, or all three. Acculturation and diffusion approaches were also useful in analyzing how the program model was disseminated to different parts of the country (for additional examples of acculturation approaches in ethnographic research, see G. Spindler, 1955; G. Spindler & Goldschmidt, 1952; L. Spindler, 1962; Tonkinson, 1974). Whereas static theories provided "snapshots" of various moments throughout the project, dynamic theories helped to identify patterns of significant behaviors over time (as part of a larger process of change).

Theories need not be elaborate juxtapositions of constructs, assumptions, propositions, and generalizations; they can be midlevel or personal theories about how the world or some small part of it works. Typically, ethnographers do not make a grand theory explicit because they do not automatically subscribe to one. A grand theory can be instructive, but many ethnographers find it unwieldy and unresponsive to day-to-day research needs. Usually, ethnographers use theoretical models indirectly linked to grand theories to guide their work. Grand theories, models, and personal theories all fall into either ideational or materialist camps—a basic dichotomy that is useful in analyzing another researcher's work and in pursuing one's own. Obviously, approaches overlap in the field, but most researchers begin by selecting a theory or model that is primarily ideational or materialist in nature before they even begin to conceptualize the problem.

The selection of a theory should depend on its appropriateness, ease of use, and explanatory power. Ideological bases for theory often blind rather than guide researchers making their way through the maze of data in the field. When theory is no longer a guide, it is no longer useful; when the data do not fit the theory, it is time to look for a new theory (for more detailed discussions of theory in ethnographic research, see Bee, 1974; Dorr-Bremme, 1985; Fetterman, 1986b; Harris, 1968; Kaplan & Manners, 1972; Pitman & Dobbert, 1986; Simon, 1986; Studstill, 1986).

RESEARCH DESIGN: FIELDWORK

The research design, according to Pelto (1970), "involves combining the essential elements of investigation into an effective problem-solving sequence" (p. 331). It is usually an idealized blueprint or road map that helps the ethnographer conceptualize how each step will follow the one before to build knowledge and understanding. The design is usually presented in the form of a proposal to solicit funds from a sponsor. The proposal will include background information, including historical information and a literature search, specific aims, rationale, methods, and significance as well as a timetable and budget. (Parts of the proposal can be reused for such products as papers, articles, final reports, and books.) A useful research design limits the scope of the endeavor, links theory to method, guides the ethnographer, and assures the sponsor.

Fieldwork is the most characteristic element of any ethnographic research design. This approach shapes the design of all ethnographic work. Classical ethnography requires from 6 months to 2 years or more in the field. Fieldwork is exploratory in nature. The ethnographer begins with a survey period to learn the basics: the native language, the kinship ties, census information, historical data, and the basic structure and function of the culture under study for the months to come. Even when the ethnographer has specific hypotheses to test in the field, information gathering proceeds inductively. (See Brim & Spain, 1974, for a discussion of hypothesis testing in anthropology.) Typically, the ethnographer generates more hypotheses than concrete findings in a study. After this survey or get-acquainted period, the ethnographer begins to draw clearer geographic and conceptual boundaries. During this postsurvey phase, the ethnographer identifies significant themes, problems, or gaps in the basic understanding of the place or program. Judgmental sampling techniques are useful in learning more about how a group thinks about the system under study. For example, in a study of conflict among the staff in a research library, I selected the most vocal and articulate group of disgruntled librarians to explain the subculture's perception of an ongoing conflict. A random sample would have been useful to depict a representative picture of the library climate, but it might have ensured that I systematically missed the most rebellious and distraught librarians. Those librarians were the ones I needed to listen to in order to understand the powerful undercurrents in the system.

In many applied settings, long-term continuous fieldwork is neither possible nor desirable. Although Malinowski's position that long-term continuous work in the field is essential applies to foreign cultures, it may be an overstatement for work conducted in one's own culture. In the CIP study mentioned previously, I visited sites for 2-week periods every few months during a 3-year study. This approach allowed me to conduct intensive fieldwork, pull back and make sense of what I had observed and recorded, and then return to the field to test my hypotheses. The effort was successful because I was able to see patterns of behavior over time. In many applied contexts, limited resources compel the researcher to apply ethnographic techniques in a contract deadline time frame rather than to conduct a full-blown ethnography.

The most important element of fieldwork is being there—to observe, to ask seemingly stupid but insightful questions, and to write down what is seen and heard. Life histories of individuals can be particularly illuminating. One articulate individual may provide a wealth of valuable information. The ethnographer must then cross-check, compare, and triangulate this information before it becomes a foundation on which to build a knowledge base. Proper organization from the beginning of the effort can facilitate this process, whether the researcher uses the traditional index cards, cardboard boxes, and lists or more high-tech databases, electronic spread sheets, word processing software, and plenty of flexible storage space for data. Keeping the data organized and handy allows the ethnographer to test minihypotheses throughout the investigation. In addition, organized, accessible data are enormously valuable when the ethnographer leaves the field and tries to put the entire puzzle together. Work conducted in the researcher's native village or country allows a second or third round of visits to check on missing information but, in most cases, it is impossible to go back. Either the culture is too far away or the program no longer exists—as is often the case with demonstration programs in evaluation research.

The decision to leave the field is based on several criteria. Often, research funding will allow only a limited amount of time in the field, thus establishing the time schedule of the research design. In other cases, either the sponsor needs information at a predetermined date or the researcher has personal and professional deadlines to meet. Of course, the best reason to leave the field is the belief that enough data have been gathered to describe the culture or problem convincingly and to say something significant about it. Different researchers require different levels of confidence about specific research findings. No one can be completely sure about the validity of research conclusions, but the ethnographer needs to gather sufficient and sufficiently accurate data to feel confident about research findings and to convince others of their accuracy. Small errors in the description of a building that houses the program under study are tolerable; basing the conceptual argument on idiosyncratic interviews is not. Finally, the law of diminishing returns can determine that it is time for the ethnographer to leave the field. When the same specific pattern of behavior emerges over and over again, the fieldworker should move on to a new topic for observation and detailed exploration. Similarly, when the general picture reaffirms itself over and over again, it is probably time to wrap things up and return home.

FORMAL ANALYSIS

Fieldwork ends when the researcher leaves the village or site, but ethnography continues. Some ethnographers spend as much time formally analyzing and reanalyzing their data and writing their ethnographies as they do conducting fieldwork. Formal analysis and report writing are more efficient when the ethnographer keeps the data organized and writes sections of the ethnography during the fieldwork. This process is much simpler in applied settings than in traditional ethnographic work because in applied settings clients expect memoranda and interim reports detailing research findings. These interim reports are the beginnings of the ethnography or ethnographically informed final report. The applied researcher also has the benefit of feedback while still in the field. A description of the group or program under study can be revised to take into account client responses about its accuracy and the ethnographer's own increasing knowledge about the program. Similarly, memoranda can be a test of the researcher's understanding of specific relationships and status symbols. During an applied study of a hospital emergency room, I wrote a memorandum describing the different types of uniforms that helicopter nurses wore compared with the traditional garb of the regular emergency nurses and suggesting that these different uniforms were status symbols that the regular nurses envied. I then concluded that this envy created friction during hospital hours (potentially affecting patient care). The response from hospital management and both sets of nurses was surprisingly positive, affirming my description and conclusions. In basic research, I have also found that sharing drafts of professional papers with informants is extremely useful. On a kibbutz in Israel, I used this technique to test my understanding of kibbutz life. Responses from kibbutz members to my observations improved the accuracy of my descriptions, insights, and findings.

In the final stage of analysis, however, the ethnographer must reconfigure all notes, memoranda, interim reports, papers, tape recordings, and so on to draw an overall picture of how a system works from myriad minute details and preliminary conclusions. This phase can be the most creative step of ethnographic research. The researcher synthesizes ideas and often makes logical leaps that lead to useful insights. Such unexpected insights are often the result of allowing the mind to wander and consider unusual combinations of thoughts. The researcher must of course backtrack to see whether the data will support these new ideas or invalidate them, but he or she will rarely achieve them through linear, methodical work alone. Conventional hard work sets the stage for these moments, but flexible thinking and what appear to be random associations are catalysts that make them happen.

THE ETHNOGRAPHY

An ethnography attempts to be holistic—covering as much territory as possible about a culture, subculture, or program—but it necessarily falls far short of the whole. An ethnographically informed report in applied studies typically has even greater limitations than an ethnography because it develops under greater time and funding constraints.

The success or failure of either report or full-blown ethnography depends on the degree to which it rings true to natives and colleagues in the field. These readers may disagree with the researcher's interpretations and conclusions, but they should recognize the details of the description as accurate. The ethnographer's task is not only to collect information from the emic or insider's perspective but also to make sense of all the data from an etic or external social scientific perspective. An ethnographer's explanation of the whole system may differ from that of the people in the field and at professional meetings. Basic descriptions of events and places, however, should sound familiar to native and colleague alike (with the logical exception of accounts of aberrant behavior or newly discovered ideas or thought processes).

Verbatim quotations are extremely useful in presenting a credible report of the research. Quotations allow the reader to judge the quality of the work—how close the ethnographer is to the thoughts of natives in the field—and to assess whether the ethnographer used such data appropriately to support the conclusions. The ethnographer therefore must select quotations that are typical or characteristic of the situation or event described. Using atypical conversations or behaviors to make one's point is not science, and the reader will probably detect the spurious nature of such material.[2]

Conveying findings in the most appropriate medium is a vital, but often overlooked, last step in ethnographic reporting. The ethnography or the ethnographically informed report is the most common medium for presenting findings. I usually include charts, pictures, and, whenever possible, computer-projected screens along with my text in presentations. Ethnographic research with policy implications in particular requires sophisticated multimedia presentations to draw an audience. In any type of research, the report or presentation must be in the language each audience understands best: "academese" for academics, "bureaucratese" for bureaucrats, plain English for most U.S. communities, and the predominant language of the people under study. Unless the ethnographer couches the research findings in language the audience understands, the most enlightening findings will fall on deaf ears. Just as learning to speak the languages of the natives under study is essential to research, learning to speak the languages of the study's multiple audiences is essential to the communication of research findings (see Fetterman, 1987a, 1987b).

The ethnography can be written in many styles and in many formats. A typical ethnography describes the history of the group, the geography of the location, kinship patterns, symbols, politics, economic systems, educational or socialization systems, and the degree of contact between the target culture and the mainstream culture.[3] Specialized ethnographies may focus on specific elements of socialization of the young or the role of a significant person such as the principal (Wolcott, 1973).

Ethnographic research findings can be communicated through newspaper releases, photographs, recordings, speech, and a variety of electronic communications. Book form, however, provides the most control over ethnographic work and remains the standard. Other forms still fall into the supplemental category.

Ethnographies usually form long but quite interesting scholarly books. Sponsors in applied settings are often more likely to read long ethnographic reports than the avalanche of figures and indecipherable statistical tables that often appear in psychometric studies. If the ethnography is too long or poorly written, however, no one but another ethnographer will read it. A lucid style and reasonable length, therefore, are critical if the ethnography is to see the light of day. I recommend a clear, easy-to-read writing style that nonacademics and readers unfamiliar with the culture or study will find interesting and understandable. Within the bounds of this rather omnibus recommendation, a multitude of writing styles exist that can interest and persuade readers of the value of an ethnographic work. In selecting a style suitable to various audiences, the ethnographer becomes rhetorician, pursuing the means of effective communication to diverse populations (Fetterman, 1987b).

BOOK ORGANIZATION

This chapter has provided a brisk walk though the intellectual landscape that this book will explore. Specifically, it has included discussion of the basic steps in ethnographic research, focusing on the selection of a problem and the use of theory. The following chapters will lead the reader step by step through the ethnographic terrain, periodically stopping to smell the roses and contemplate the value of one concept or technique over another.

Chapter 2 focuses on guiding concepts in ethnography: culture, cultural interpretation, emic and etic perspectives, a nonjudgmental orientation, inter- and intracultural diversity, structure and function, and ritual and symbols as well as micro and macro approaches and operationalism. Chapter 3 presents the specific data collection methods and techniques necessary for conducting an ethnography. Methods and techniques under discussion include fieldwork, selection and sampling, gaining entry, participant observation, interviewing (structured, semistructured, informal, and retrospective), survey or grand tour questions, specific questions (such as structural and attribute questions), open-ended and closed-ended questions, interviewing protocols and strategies, key actor or informant interviewing, gathering of life histories and expressive autobiographical interviews, use of lists and forms, questionnaires, projective techniques, and various unobtrusive measures.

Ethnographic research equipment is discussed in Chapter 4. The most important piece of equipment is the human instrument—the ethnographer. Other common tools include pen and notepad, laptop and desktop computers with accompanying software, Internet search engines and web pages, tape recorder, camera, videotape camera and VCR, and cinema. These tools facilitate the ethnographic mission. They are used to collect, organize, store, analyze, and present the data. Chapter 5 explores the role of analysis throughout ethnography. The process includes a discussion of seemingly simple thought processes and more time-consuming and labor-intensive processes, such as triangulation, documentation of thought and behavior patterns, and key event analysis. In addition, it discusses diagrams, flowcharts, organizational charts, matrices, content analysis, and statistics.

Chapter 6 describes ethnographic writing. Writing, like analysis, occurs throughout the ethnographic endeavor. Specific milestones highlight the significance of writing in ethnography, including the research proposal, field notes, memoranda, interim reports, final reports, articles, and books. Fundamental elements of ethnographic style are also examined, such as thick description, verbatim quotations, the use of the ethnographic present, and ethnographic presence. The chapter discusses ethnographically informed reports and the role of literature and various editorial concerns.

Chapter 7, the last step in our hike through the ethnographic landscape, presents a discussion of ethics, focusing on the conceptual crossroads of methods and ethics in ethnographic research. Ethics, like analysis and writing, cut across every step in the ethnographer's path. The selection of a problem to study and the choice of an academic or applied role have ethical implications for each stage of the study—from inception to publication. Basic underlying ethical standards include the securing of permission (to protect individual privacy), honesty, trust (both implicit and explicit), reciprocity, and rigorous work. More sophisticated ethical dilemmas in ethnographic research include guilty knowledge and dirty hands.

Each chapter builds on the one before—as each step on a path follows the step before. The discussion about the selection of a problem and the role of theory in this chapter is followed by a detailed discussion of guiding concepts in Chapter 2. The ethnographer's next logical step is to become acquainted with the tools of the trade—the methods and techniques required to conduct ethnographic research and the equipment used to chisel out this scientific art form. A discussion of analysis in ethnographic research becomes more meaningful at this stage, once the preceding chapters have laid the foundation for this discussion. Similarly, the role of writing is discussed in Chapter 6 because writing is one of the final stages in the process and because the meaning of writing in ethnography is amplified and made more illuminating by a series of discussions about what "doing ethnography" entails. Finally, ethics is discussed last because the complete ethnographic context is necessary to a meaningful discussion of this topic. Step by step, the chapters provide a path through the complex terrain of ethnographic work. Newcomers will be able to proceed chapter by chapter toward an overall understanding of ethnography. Experienced ethnographers will find that the chapters offer self-contained reference points for refreshment and enjoyment.

NOTES

1. Arguably, Radcliffe-Brown's (1952) functionalism is static and Vogt's (1960) and Geertz's (1957) is dynamic, but both forms are static in comparison to most conventional dynamic theories.

2. A researcher may select quotations that reflect political ideology or altruistic intentions. This course, however, is an overzealous commitment to a cause and not science. The line between good conscientious research and political advocacy is thin, but when the researcher crosses it the quality and integrity of the research are compromised. A good researcher is not afraid to enter the political arena—after completing the research.

3. An ethnography is primarily descriptive in nature. An ethnology compares and contrasts cultures and cultural elements. Ethnology relies on ethnographies as the primary data. An ethnography and an ethnology are both used to complete a comprehensive anthropological study, requiring the conventional literature review, presentation of data collection techniques, description, interpretation, and discussion of implications. An ethnography is the descriptive tool in anthropology that can stand alone or be the foundation for larger efforts.

2

Walking in Rhythm: Anthropological Concepts

*Heard melodies are sweet,
but those unheard are sweeter;
therefore, ye soft pipes, play on.*

—John Keats

Ethnography is what ethnographers actually do in the field. Textbooks such as this one, Pelto (1970), Pelto and Pelto's (1978) exemplary work, Spradley (1979, 1980), Spradley and McCurdy (1972, 1975), Werner and Schoepfle (1987a, 1987b), Goetz and LeCompte (1984), Agar (1980, 1986), and many others—together with lectures—can initiate the newcomer to the field and refresh the experienced ethnographer, but actual fieldwork experience has no substitute. A well-trained ethnographer balances formal education, including textbooks and classroom instruction, with time in the field (Lareau, 1987). How the ethnographer conducts a study speaks most precisely to the question of what is ethnography.

This chapter introduces some of the most important concepts that guide ethnographers in their fieldwork. As the title suggests, these concepts can set the rhythm and stride of the fieldwork—much as music can help a hiker develop a rhythmic, smooth pace that speeds the journey and eases strain (for a discussion of rhythm and pace, see Fletcher, 1970, pp. 47-52). With experience, these concepts become automatic, guiding the ethnographer's strategy and behavior in the field. This chapter will help to socialize the new ethnographer into the culture under study through a focus on fundamental ethnographic concepts and research values. In conjunction with Chapter 3, which discusses methods and techniques, this discussion should also help the initiate use the right tools for each task—at the right time. Experienced ethnographers will recognize parallels to their own knowledge. A discussion of the folklore of fieldwork and the instruments of the trade can help to crystallize their experience and refine their skills.

CULTURE

Culture is the broadest ethnographic concept. Definitions of culture typically espouse either a materialist or an ideational perspective. The classic materialist interpretation of culture focuses on behavior. In this view, culture is the sum of a social group's observable patterns of behavior, customs, and way of life (Harris, 1968, p. 16). The most popular ideational definition of culture is the cognitive definition. According to the cognitive approach, culture comprises the ideas, beliefs, and knowledge that characterize a particular group of people. This second—and currently most popular—definition specifically excludes behavior. Obviously, ethnographers need to know about both cultural behavior and knowledge to describe a culture or subculture adequately. Although neither definition is sufficient, each offers the ethnographer a starting point and a perspective from which to approach the group under study. For example, adopting a cognitive definition of culture would orient the ethnographer toward linguistic data: daily discourse. A cognitive ethnographer would ask members of the social group how they define their reality, what the subcategories of their existence are, and what their symbols mean. This cognitive researcher might create taxonomies to distinguish among levels and categories of meaning. Both material and ideational definitions are useful at different times in exploring fully how groups of people think and behave in their natural environment.

However defined, the concept of culture helps the ethnographer search for a logical, cohesive pattern in the myriad, often ritualistic behaviors and ideas that characterize a group. This concept becomes immediately meaningful after cross-cultural experience. Everything is new to a student first entering a different culture. Attitudes or habits that natives espouse virtually without thinking are distinct and clear to the stranger. Living in a foreign community for a long period of time enables the fieldworker to see the power of dominant ideas, values, and patterns of behavior in the way people walk, talk, dress, eat, and sleep. The longer an individual stays in a community, building rapport, and the deeper the probe into individual lives, the greater the probability of his or her learning about the sacred subtle elements of the culture: how people pray, how they feel about each other, and how they reinforce their own cultural practices to maintain the integrity of their system. Interestingly, living and working in another culture helps one to objectify the behaviors and beliefs not only of people in a foreign culture but also of individuals in one's native culture. After a period away, the returning ethnographer often feels like a stranger in a strange land—in the midst of what is most familiar. This experience is often referred to as "culture shock."

Anthropologists learn about the intricacies of a subgroup or community to describe it in all its richness and complexity. In the process of studying these details, they typically discover underlying forces that make the system tick. These cultural elements are values or beliefs that can unite or divide a group but that are commonly shared focal points. An awareness of what role these abstract elements play in a given culture can give the researcher a clearer picture of how the culture works. For example, each culture has a specific kinship structure and religious and economic practices. These elements of culture operate unnoticed in day-to-day situations—much as grammar operates in language. Different subgroups in a culture may have widely disparate attitudes about the surface level of their kinship, religious, and economic systems, but they generally share a common belief in the deeper, often subconscious meaning behind these culture elements. For example, a young American couple might argue about whether the woman will assume the man's name when they marry. The fact that they need to argue the question indicates an underlying kinship system in which the woman and any children traditionally adopt the man's name. Thus, although the two disagree about their future name (or names), they acknowledge in their discussion the dominance of the kinship system known as patrilineal descent and a shared focal point of interaction and underlying assumptions about traditionally shared beliefs and behavior (for additional discussion about kinship and social organization, see Bohannan & Middleton, 1968).[1]

Many anthropologists consider cultural interpretation ethnography's primary contribution. Cultural interpretation involves the ability to describe what the researcher has heard and seen within the framework of the social group's view of reality. A classic example of the interpretive contribution involves the wink and the blink. A mechanical difference between the two may not be evident. The cultural context of each movement, the relationship between individuals that each act suggests, and the contexts surrounding the two, however, help define and differentiate these two significantly different behaviors. Anyone who has ever mistaken a blink for a wink is fully aware of the significance of cultural interpretation (Fetterman, 1982a, p. 24; Geertz, 1973, p. 6; Wolcott, 1980, pp. 57, 59).

A cultural interpretation rests on a foundation of carefully collected ethnographic data. Together with ethnographic methods and techniques, cultural interpretation and a variety of other fundamental concepts shape what ethnography is—notably, a holistic perspective, contextualization, and emic, etic, and nonjudgmental views of reality.

HOLISTIC PERSPECTIVE

Ethnographers assume a holistic outlook in research to gain a comprehensive and complete picture of a social group. Ethnographers attempt to describe as much as possible about a culture or a social group. This description might include the group's history, religion, politics, economy, and environment. No study can capture an entire culture or group. The holistic orientation forces the fieldworker to see beyond an immediate cultural scene or event in a classroom, hospital room, city street, or plush offices in Washington, D.C., New York, or Chicago. Each scene exists within a multilayered and interrelated context.

A holistic orientation demands a great deal of time in the field to gather the many kinds of data that together create a picture of the social whole. It also requires multiple methods and multiple hypotheses to ensure that the researcher covers all angles. Ideally, this orientation can help the fieldworker discover the interrelationships among the various systems and subsystems in a community or program under study—generally through an emphasis on the contextualization of data.

CONTEXTUALIZATION

Contextualizing data involves placing observations into a larger perspective. For example, in my Career Intern Program (CIP) study (see Chapter 1), I observed that very little was happening in one of the four drop-out programs. Students spent time hanging around outside the school building. Some teachers were absent for days at a time. The program lacked the studious atmosphere present in other sites. A description that merely recounted events on the classroom or school level would have depicted a failed program unable to motivate its teachers or students. When I asked students why they were not in class, however, they said that the program had no class materials to work on—"not even no paper." I then began to track down the cause of the shortage by interviewing the teachers. They indicated that they were receiving no funds for classroom materials. After probing one administrative level after another, I finally traced the problem to an argument between the program's federal sponsor and its federal monitor or managing agency. The managing agency said that the sponsor owed the agency money and told the sponsor that it would not disperse funds for the drop-out program until the money was paid. The fallout from this interagency rivalry reached the classroom and brought the program to a virtual halt. This information provided the broader context necessary to produce a classroom description from a policy perspective.

By combining those data with a brief description of the inner-city environment in which the schools were located—an impoverished neighborhood in which pimping, prostitution, arson for hire, rape, and murder were commonplace—I produced a report that helped policymakers understand the power of certain elements in the community to distract students from their studies. This description also provided some insight into the often lucrative alternatives with which the school competed in attracting and keeping students. Contextualization thus prevented me and the program sponsors from making the common mistake of blaming the victim (Fetterman, 1981b).

In another example drawn from this study, policymakers were contemplating terminating one drop-out program because of its low attendance—approximately 60% to 70%. My reminder that the baseline with which to compare 60% to 70% attendance was zero attendance—these were students who systematically skipped school—helped the policymakers make a more informed decision about the program. In this case, contextualization ensured that the program would continue serving former dropouts (Fetterman, 1987a).

EMIC PERSPECTIVE
AND MULTIPLE REALITIES

The emic perspective—the insider's or native's perspective of reality—is at the heart of most ethnographic research. The insider's perception of reality is instrumental to understanding and accurately describing situations and behaviors. Native perceptions may not conform to an "objective" reality, but they help the fieldworker understand why members of the social group do what they do. In contrast to a priori assumptions about how systems work from a simple, linear, logical perspective—which might be completely off target—ethnography typically takes a phenomenologically oriented research approach.

An emic perspective compels the recognition and acceptance of multiple realities. Documenting multiple perspectives of reality in a given study is crucial to an understanding of why people think and act in the different ways they do. Differing perceptions of reality can be useful clues to individuals' religious, economic, or political status and can help a researcher understand maladaptive behavior patterns. For example, in one study of a folk medicating group, eliciting the emic perspective and acknowledging multiple realities helped me discover why so many deaths had occurred in the community. I learned that the group members often relied on native curers or *curanderos* to heal them with herbs, prayers, medallions, candles, statues, incense, soaps, aerosols, and money. The Seven African Powers is one of the most popular constellations of prayer, ritual, candles, and talismans. The seven saints of the African Powers are *chango, orula, ogum, elegua, obatala, yemalla,* and *ochun.* Each represents a specific force and is represented by specific amulets, herbs, incense, and oil (for examples of religious instructional material, see Claremont, 1938; Gamache, 1942).

The folk medicators had an elaborate explanation for illness and healing that conflicted with the beliefs and practices of conventional Western medicine. Members of this group, however, were also seeing Western physicians—a large leap of faith and a critical juncture in the socialization and assimilation process. Some of these people believed their folk medications were not as effective as they used to be, and others were simply persuaded by children or friends to visit physicians. The latter group saw folk medications as effective and Western medicine as ineffective. They saw physicians to avoid arguments with their children or out of respect for friends; they assumed that modern medicine was worthless and probably could not hurt them. They were too embarrassed to tell their Western physicians about their folk medicating practices, however, and many of their physicians either did not want to hear about those practices or dismissed them out of hand. Because they were caught between two conflicting medical traditions, the members of this social group resolved their conflict by taking their folk medications and their physicians' prescriptions at the same time. The results ranged from disillusionment with modern medicine to death. The two medical traditions overlapped with sometimes lethal effects. The folk medicators were taking strong herbs, including foxglove, which contains digitalis (a heart stimulant). Patients who were also taking prescription digitalis received a fatal overdose of the stimulant.

The study sensitized folk medicators and physicians to each other's subcultures, thus reducing the mortality rate. It also demonstrated the significance of assuming the emic perspective and acknowledging multiple realities. In this study, however, the different realities (folk medicators and physicians) were in conflict and required an etic or outsider's perspective to form a complete picture of this medical and cultural phenomenon.

ETIC PERSPECTIVE

An etic perspective is the external, social scientific perspective on reality. Some ethnographers are interested only in describing the emic view, without placing their data in an etic or scientific perspective. They stand at the ideational and phenomenological end of the ethnographic spectrum. Other ethnographers prefer to rely on etically derived data first and consider emically derived data secondary in their analysis. They stand at the materialist and positivistic philosophical end of the ethnographic spectrum. At one time, a conflict about whether the causes of human actions are motivated primarily by ideas (ideational, typically emically oriented perspective) or by the environment (materialist, often etically based perspective) consumed the field. Today, most ethnographers simply see emic and etic orientations as markers along a continuum of styles or different levels of analysis. Most ethnographers start collecting data from the emic perspective and then try to make sense of what they have collected in terms of both the native's view and their own scientific analysis. Just as thorough fieldwork requires an insightful and sensitive cultural interpretation combined with rigorous data collection techniques, good ethnography requires both emic and etic perspectives.

I always ground my work in an emic understanding of the situation and group. Satisfactorily eliciting, recording, and expressing this perspective takes hours, days, months, and sometimes years. Although time-consuming, this approach ensures the validity and usefulness of the data I have collected. At the same time, the job is not done until I step back and make sense of the situation from both emic and etic perspectives. Chapter 3 will discuss many of the tools used to collect and interpret data. Chapter 5 will discuss analyzing reams of data from emic and etic perspectives.

NONJUDGMENTAL ORIENTATION

Some ethnographic concepts push the researcher to explore in new directions, some ensure that the data are valid, and others simply prevent contamination of the data. A nonjudgmental orientation helps ethnographers on all three fronts. Most important, this concept prevents ethnographers from making inappropriate and unnecessary value judgments about what they observe.

A nonjudgmental orientation requires the ethnographer to suspend personal valuation of any given cultural practice. Maintaining a nonjudgmental orientation is similar to suspending disbelief while one watches a movie or play or reads a book—one accepts what may be an obviously illogical or unbelievable set of circumstances to allow the author to unravel a riveting story.

An experience I had with the Bedouin Arabs in the Sinai desert provides a useful example of this conceptual guideline. During my stay with the Bedouins, I tried not to let my bias for Western hygiene practices and monogamy surface in my interactions or writings. I say "tried" because my reaction to one of my first acquaintances, a Bedouin with a leathery face and feet, was far from neutral. I was astonished. I admired his ability to survive and adapt in a harsh environment, moving from one water hole to the next throughout the desert. My personal reaction to the odor of his garments (particularly after a camel ride), however, was far from impartial. He shared his jacket with me to protect me from the heat. I thanked him, of course, because I appreciated the gesture and did not want to insult him. I smelled like a camel for the rest of the day in the dry desert heat, however. I thought I did not need the jacket because we were only a kilometer or two from our destination, Saint Catherine's monastery, but the short trip took forever—up rocky paths and down through *wadis* or valleys. I learned later that without his jacket, I would have suffered from sunstroke. The desert heat is so dry that perspiration evaporates almost immediately, and an inexperienced traveler does not always notice when the temperature climbs above 130° Fahrenheit. By slowing down the evaporation rate, the jacket helped me retain water. Had I rejected his jacket and, by implication, Bedouin hygiene practices, I would have baked, and I would never have understood how much their lives revolve around water, the desert's most precious resource. Our seemingly circuitous ride followed a hidden water route, not a straight line, to the monastery.

The point, simply, is that ethnographers must attempt to view another culture without making value judgments about unfamiliar practices, but ethnographers cannot be completely neutral. We are all products of our culture. We have personal beliefs, biases, and individual tastes. Socialization runs deep. The ethnographer can guard against the more obvious biases, however, by making them explicit and by trying to view another culture's practices impartially. Ethnocentric behavior—the imposition of one culture's values and standards on another culture, with the assumption that one is superior to the other—is a fatal error in ethnography.

INTER- AND INTRACULTURAL DIVERSITY

One danger of ethnography is that it can produce a stereotype of a group, subculture, or culture. The ethnographer must reduce and crystallize a world of observation to produce a clear picture of a community. As long and detailed as most ethnographies are, they typically represent only a fraction of what the ethnographer learned and saw. Holistic, contextual, emic, etic, and nonjudgmental concepts require the ethnographer to boil down all the information, observations, interviews, theories, and patterns that emerge during fieldwork to produce the essence of a culture.

These concepts are at once restricting and liberating. They stretch one's perceptual talents to the limit, enabling the ethnographer to see familiar events in a new light and to notice previously unnoticed details of behavior and routine. At the same time, these pressures shape the ethnographer's every move, much as natural factors such as the weather and the contours of rock shape a rock climber's every move. The rock climber must concentrate, searching for the best crack in which to wedge a hand or a foot and the best position from which to work a way up the rock. The sheer drop, stray gusts of wind, and the contours of the rock direct and limit the climber's moves to the top. Similarly, the fieldworker must grab hold of and work a way through what is said and done throughout fieldwork. These concepts shape data collection and analysis, and they prevent the researcher from either drowning in detail or missing subtle differences in the quest for the big picture.

The concepts of inter- and intracultural diversity are particularly useful here. *Intercultural diversity* refers to the differences between two cultures, and *intracultural diversity* refers to the differences between subcultures within a culture. Intercultural differences are reasonably easy to see. Compare the descriptions of two different cultures on a point-by-point basis—their political, religious, economic, kinship, and ecological systems and other pertinent dimensions. Intracultural differences, however, are more likely to go unnoticed. An early effort of mine to describe an inner-city school at which I taught as a teacher-researcher excluded much of the neighborhood's diversity. Friends in the community reviewed a draft, and their comments made me realize the simplicity of my description. I had described the torn-down buildings, the drunks and addicts on the street, the factory-like schools, and the crime. I had failed to mention, however, the small but vocal minority who were trying to revitalize the inner city. Some houses were newly painted, a newly organized parents' association was attempting to deal with juvenile delinquents, and a community club had developed. I had missed an important segment of the population. These people were in the minority, but they did have an impact on the community. No group is completely homogeneous. In my zeal to conceptualize and communicate the big picture, I failed to see and share the differences—the intracultural diversity. Thus, my big picture was not the whole picture. The revised draft was a more balanced report that gave the big picture more credibility and was a closer approximation of the whole.

These concepts place a check on our observations. They help the fieldworker see differences that may invalidate pat theories or hypotheses about observed events in the field. In some cases, these differences are systematic patterned activities for a broad spectrum of the community, compelling the fieldworker to readjust the research focus; to throw away dated and inappropriate theories, models, hypotheses, and assumptions; and to modify the vision of the finished puzzle. In other cases, the differences are idiosyncratic but useful in underscoring another, dominant pattern—the exception that proves the rule. In most cases, however, such differences are instructive about a level or dimension of the community that had not received sufficient consideration (for an illustration of intracultural diversity in qualitative research, see Fetterman, 1988b).

STRUCTURE AND FUNCTION

Structure and function are traditional concepts that guide research in social organization. *Structure* here refers to the social structure or configuration of the group, such as the kinship or political structure. *Function* refers to the social relations among members of the group. Most groups have an identifiable internal structure and an established set of social relationships that help regulate behavior. For example, a corporation typically has a formal organizational chart depicting the company's hierarchical structure and various subgroups. A corporate organizational chart presents an idealized image of the company and can be a useful starting point for the ethnographer studying corporate culture. The chart is itself a statement about the nature of the organization. The ethnographer's task, however, requires a more penetrating inquiry into the informal networks and influences governing the corporation. The ethnographer must describe the underlying structure of an organization to understand its inner workings. This process is much like discovering and separating the surface from the deep level of meaning in language. The ethnographer must also describe the functional relationship of one part of an organization to another to explain how the sociocultural system operates.

Unlike corporations, most cultures and subcultures rarely have explicit organizational charts detailing their structure, functional relationships, and interrelationships. Even inner-city gangs, however, have observable patterns: After documenting behavior patterns during fights within the gang and between various gangs, as well as various economic exchanges, the urban ethnographer learns the leaders of the groups, the network of elaborate allegiances, and the obvious functional relationships. The functional relationship between gang members stealing property and those fencing stolen property is vital to gang economic survival. Similarly, allegiances arising from warring groups over disputes related to these economic exchanges are also apparent. (See Evans-Pritchard, 1940, for a discussion of segmentary linkages and Keiser, 1969, as they relate to inner-city gangs.)

Ethnographers use the concepts of structure and function to guide their inquiry. They extract information from the group under study to construct a skeletal structure and then thread in the social functions—the muscle, flesh, and nerves that fill out the skeleton. A detailed understanding of the underlying structure of a system provides the ethnographer with a foundation on and frame within which to construct an ethnographic description.[2]

SYMBOL AND RITUAL

Ethnographers look for symbols that help them understand and describe a culture. Symbols are condensed expressions of meaning that evoke powerful feelings and thoughts. A cross or a menorah represents an entire religion, and a swastika represents a movement, whether the original Nazi movement or one of the many neo-Nazi movements. A flag represents an entire country, evoking both patriotic fervor and epithets.

Symbols, however, are not limited to nations, large-scale organizations, and movements; they are part of everyday life. Schools select a mascot to embody school spirit. Members of social or academic fraternities wear pins to identify themselves. Symbols provide the ethnographer with insight into a culture and a tool with which to further probe various cultural beliefs and practices. Symbols are often part of a ritual. Rituals are repeated patterns of symbolic behavior that play a part in both religious and secular life. In the CIP school, administrators, teachers, and students wore a special school T-shirt 1 day a month every month. The T-shirt represented the program's values of cooperation, hard work, friendship, achievement, and educational opportunity.

The dropout's T-shirt, as a symbol, was worn every month on a special day. The day was a program ritual in which students received special awards to reinforce specific positive behaviors—for example, an award for best or most improved attendance. Everyone in the program, including the principal, wore the symbolic T-shirt during this rite of solidarity. The ritual served to reinforce the group's unity or family feeling as well as to reward desirable behaviors (for another illustration, see Burnett, 1976). Rituals also exist in business organizations and institutions. During a study of a university hospital, I found that one administrator examined the budget and expense statement every month. She would check every line item to see if every charge had a receipt. Hers was a ritualistic behavior. In this case, however, the ritual was hollow and had lost all meaning. The administrator checked for the appropriate receipts for all expenses but never checked to see if the charges themselves were appropriate. In many cases, charges were completely inappropriate. The ritual gave her and the hospital a false sense of security and convinced the hospital administration that it had a firm grip on finances despite the hospital's rapid expansion and growing complexity (Fetterman, 1986e).

Ethnographers view symbols and rituals as a form of cultural shorthand. Symbols open doors to initial understanding and crystallize critical cultural knowledge. Together, they help ethnographers make sense of observations by providing a framework in which to classify and categorize behavior (Dolgin, Kemnitzer, & Schneider, 1977).

MICRO- OR MACROLEVEL STUDY

The application of these concepts to ethnographic work does not take place in a vacuum. The ethnographer's orientation is determined by the study's boundaries. In turn, these boundaries evolve from the study itself. Some basic parameters, however, can be established at the beginning of the study.

An ethnographer's theoretical disposition and problem selection will determine whether a micro- or macrolevel study is conducted. A microlevel study is a close-up view, as if under a microscope, of a small social unit or an identifiable activity within the social unit. Typically, an ethnomethodologist or symbolic interactionist will conduct a microanalysis. For example, Erickson's (1976) study of gatekeepers involved reviewing videotaped recordings of interviews to study the subtle signals counselors gave to their clients.

The areas of proxemics and kinesics in anthropology involve microlevel studies. Proxemics is the study of how the socially defined physical distance between people varies in differing social circumstances. For example, a stranger standing 3 inches away from you and shouting obscenities is clearly violating an American sense of appropriate distance unless the incident occurs at a hockey game or a heavy metal rock concert (Hall, 1974). Kinesics is the study of body language. A motorcyclist who gives "the bird" to a motorist who ran him off the road is communicating a clear social message—and participating in a form of cultural communication or, more specifically, body language (Birdwhistell, 1970).

In the CIP study, I performed a microanalysis of one example of classroom behavior. I took a series of pictures of a brief encounter between a teacher and a student. I took 10 photographs in 30 seconds every 10 minutes. During one of the more vivid cultural scenes, the student was summoned by the teacher to go over the previous night's assignment, while the other students continued to work on their own projects. The student had not done the work and did not want to go up to the teacher. The teacher knew the student had not completed the assignment, just as he knew the student had not completed every other assignment that month. The photographs document the student pulling himself together reluctantly to do battle with the teacher. With a sigh and a deep breath, he slowly pulled himself out of his chair to go to the teacher's desk. The teacher—tired and demonstrably disinterested in this particular student—changed his facial expression from withdrawal to feigned interest. The photographs document the tension between the two as the meeting developed into a brief shouting match and subsided, concluding in a draw in which both fighters went back to their corners until the next round. This particular scene transpired in less than a minute. This microlevel of documentation can constitute a study in itself or, as in this case, highlight one element of a study.

Shultz and Florio (1979) provide a useful example of a microlevel study of an entire classroom. They demonstrated how a teacher used social and physical space to orchestrate classroom activity. They collected 70 hours of videotape of classroom activity during a 2-year period. The second year of the study also involved observation of the classroom to inform their interpretation of the videotapes. Wolcott's (1973) *The Man in the Principal's Office* focuses on a single occupation within the school system (without videotapes) and represents a spectacular microethnography (Basham & DeGroot, 1977, p. 428; Wolcott, 1982, p. 90).

A macrolevel study focuses on the large picture. In anthropology, the large picture can range from a single school to worldwide systems. The typical ethnography focuses on a community or specific sociocultural system. Spindler and Spindler's series, *Case Studies in Cultural Anthro-*

pology, provides some of the best examples of contemporary ethnographies. They include studies of the Yanomamo (Chagnon, 1977), Dinka (Deng, 1972), Amish (Hostetler & Huntington, 1971), Hutterites (Hostetler & Huntington, 1967), Tiwi (Australian aborigines) (Hart & Pilling, 1960), Navajo (Downs, 1972), Blackfeet (McFee, 1972), Krsna (Daner, 1976), and even a retirement community (Jacobs, 1974). Some of the best educational ethnographies in the series include a study of a residential school for Indian children (King, 1967) and one of an elementary school in Harlem (Rosenfeld, 1971). Each study attempts to describe an entire cultural group—its way of life and social and cultural systems. Clearly, a researcher who conducts either a micro- or macrolevel study can connect the findings of that study to the next larger system that affects it. (See Ogbu, 1978, for a successful example of a multilevel ethnography.) The link between a fine-grained microlevel study and a broad study of corporate America, for example, is a difficult stretch. In fact, generalizing from most macrolevel studies is difficult. Ethnographic work, whether at the microlevel or macrolevel, involves detailed description. The decision to undertake a micro- or macrolevel study is partially a function of the ethnographer's talents or proclivities. Some ethnographers are better at detailed frame-by-frame analysis of events or parts of events. Other ethnographers are more interested in larger sets of observable interrelationships with potentially greater generalizability. Microlevel studies require as much time to conduct as macrolevel studies; an ethnographer conducting a microlevel study, however, can spend as much time on one facet of a social event as another researcher spends conducting a macrolevel study involving 20 different people in 10 social settings. The selection of a micro- or macrolevel of study depends on what the researcher wants to know and, thus, what theory the study involves and how the researcher has defined the problem under study.

OPERATIONALISM

One of the more focused concepts in fieldwork is that of operationalism. A discussion of operationalism is as much a call for it as it is an indication of the direction ethnography is taking. Simply, *operationalism* means defining one's terms and methods of measurement. In simple descriptive accounts, saying that "a few people said this and a few others said that" may not be problematic. Establishing a significant relationship between facts and theory or interpreting "the facts," however, requires greater specificity. For example, the statement, "Hostility increases when too many students are in the class" may be a perfectly accurate observation. Several questions arise, however: What constitutes hostility? How is an increase of hostility measured? How many is too many students in a class? On a simpler level, sentences beginning "Some of them believe" are commonplace. Being more specific—citing the specific sources and the exact nature of their "belief"—is not difficult and conveys more information and greater credibility and validity. Operationalism tests us and forces us to be honest with ourselves. Instead of leaving conclusions to strong impressions, the fieldworker should quantify or identify the source of ethnographic insights whenever possible. Specifying how one arrives at one's conclusions gives other researchers something concrete to use and something to prove or disprove. It is impossible to operationalize everything—the job of doing ethnography would never be done. Much can be done to increase recording and reporting accuracy, however.

Many concepts in ethnography help to explain what ethnography is all about and to guide an ethnographer in the pursuit of a study. This chapter has provided a discussion of some of the most important concepts in the profession, beginning with such global concepts as culture, a holistic orientation, and contextualization and gradually shifting to more narrow concepts—inter- and intracultural diversity, structure and function, symbol and ritual, and operationalism. Chapter 3 details the ethnographic methods and techniques that grow out of these concepts and allow the researcher to carry out the work of ethnography.

NOTES

1. Anthropologists typically focus on this cultural level, in contrast to sociologists, who generally focus on society. As fieldworkers, both anthropologists and sociologists require detailed information about the groups they study to generate their findings and insights. The lenses through which they view the data are different, however. Ethnographers come from an anthropological tradition and thus rely on the culture concept to guide their research. Note, however, that many sociologists today have cultural concerns, and many anthropologists focus on societal concerns. The research traditions of each discipline, however, shape the respective researchers' behaviors and thoughts. In addition, the culture concept—whether employed by a sociologist or by an anthropologist—is useful and, for better or worse, part of the conceptual baggage an ethnographer carries into the field.

2. Using an inductive approach, ethnographers describe the function of each part of a culture to understand better how the culture works as a whole. The concepts of structure and function are useful heuristic tools with which to understand and elaborate the basic elements of a culture.

3

A Wilderness Guide: Methods and Techniques

*To a person uninstructed in natural history, his country or seaside stroll
is a walk through a gallery filled with wonderful works of art,
nine-tenths of which have their faces turned to the wall.*

—Thomas Huxley

The ethnographer is a human instrument. With a research problem, a
theory of social interaction or behavior, and a variety of conceptual
guidelines in mind, the ethnographer strides into a culture or social
situation to explore its terrain and to collect and analyze data. Relying
on all its senses, thoughts, and feelings, the human instrument is a most
sensitive and perceptive data gathering tool. The information this tool
gathers, however, can be subjective and misleading. Fieldworkers may
lose their bearings in the maze of unfamiliar behaviors and situations.
Ethnographic methods and techniques help to guide the ethnographer
through the wilderness of personal observation and to identify and
classify accurately the bewildering variety of events and actions that
form a social situation. The ethnographer's hike through the social and
cultural wilderness begins with fieldwork.

FIELDWORK

Fieldwork is the hallmark of research for both sociologists and anthropologists. The method is essentially the same for both types of researchers—
working with people for long periods of time in their natural setting. The
ethnographer conducts research in the native environment to see people
and their behavior given all the real-world incentives and constraints. This
naturalist approach avoids the artificial response typical of controlled or
laboratory conditions. Understanding the world—or some small fragment

31

of it—requires studying it in all its wonder and complexity. The task is in many ways more difficult than laboratory study, but it can also be more rewarding.

The fieldworker uses a variety of methods and techniques to ensure the integrity of the data. These methods and techniques objectify and standardize the researcher's perceptions. Of course, the ethnographer must adapt each one of the methods and techniques discussed in this chapter to the local environment. Resource constraints and deadlines may also limit the length of time for data gathering in the field—exploring, cross-checking, and recording information.

SELECTION AND SAMPLING

The research questions shape the selection of a place and a people or program to study. For example, the probability of finding relevant data about the relationship between educational mechanisms, such as teacher expectations, and school success or failure is higher in a classroom than in a board of education meeting, although the latter setting has relevance as well. The ideal site for investigation of the research problem is not always accessible. In that event, the researcher accepts and notes the limitations of the study from the onset. Ideally, the focus of the investigation shifts to match the site under study. If either the match or the problem is not credible, the researcher may have to abandon the initial study and develop new research questions. In contract research, a contract modification might be necessary as well. This process may jeopardize the study's funding, but in some instances it is the only intellectually honest step to take.

The next step is to decide how to sample members of the target population. There are two approaches to this decision. First, choose who and what not to study. This process of elimination is like the admissions process at topflight universities and colleges. The decision is not who shall we admit but rather who must we reject—given all the people who qualify. An unwieldy number of informative people and useful events present themselves for study. The researcher must filter out those sources of information that will add little to the study. Second, select who and what to study—that is, the sources that will most help to understand life in a given community.

Most ethnographers use the big-net approach conducive to participant observation—mixing and mingling with everyone they can at first. As the study progresses, the focus narrows to specific portions of the population under study. The big-net approach ensures a wide-angle view of events before the microscopic study of specific interactions begins. This big picture helps refine an ethnographer's focus and aids the fieldworker in understanding the finer details that he or she will capture on film and in notes for further analysis.

Ethnographers typically use an informal strategy to begin fieldwork, such as starting wherever they can slip a foot in the door. The most common technique is judgmental sampling—that is, ethnographers rely on their judgment to select the most appropriate members of the subculture or unit based on the research question. This approach is quite natural, requiring the ethnographer to ask very simple, direct questions about what people do. Natural opportunities, convenience, and luck also play a part in the process if the ethnographer is savvy enough to make good use of them. Some experienced ethnographers use a rigorous randomized strategy to begin work—particularly when they already know a great deal about the culture or unit they are studying.

Using a highly structured randomized design without a basic understanding of the people under study may cause the researcher to narrow the focus prematurely, thus eliminating perhaps the very people or subjects relevant to the study. Such a misdirected study may yield high reliability but extremely low validity, undermining an entire research study. First the ethnographer must ask the right questions for a given research study. The best way to learn how to ask the right questions—beyond the literature search and proposal ideas—is to go into the field and find out what people do day to day. Goetz and LeCompte (1984, pp. 63-84) provide a useful discussion of sampling and selection in ethnographic research, focusing on criterion-based and probabilistic sampling.

ENTRY

An introduction by a member is the ethnographer's best ticket into the community. Walking into a community cold can have a chilling effect on ethnographic research. Community members may not be interested in the individual ethnographer or in the work. An intermediary or go-between can open doors otherwise locked to outsiders. The facilitator may be a chief, principal, director, teacher, tramp, or gang member and should have some credibility with the group—either as a member or as an acknowledged friend or associate. The closer the go-between's ties to the group the better. The trust the group places in the intermediary will approximate the trust it extends to the ethnographer at the beginning of the study. Ethnographers thus benefit from a halo effect if they are introduced by the right person: Sight unseen, group members will give the researcher the benefit of the doubt. As long as ethnographers demonstrate that they deserve the group's trust, they will probably do well. A strong recommendation and introduction strengthen the fieldworker's capacity to work in a community and thus improve the quality of the data.

Unfortunately, the fieldworker cannot always find the best person to offer an introduction and must take whatever is available. In this case, the researcher must consider entering the community without assistance—simply by walking into a neighborhood store, attending church services, volunteering time in a school, or performing any other nonthreatening role in the community. In many instances, however, access is clearly impossible without some escort. Here, the fieldworker must accept a devil's bargain—a poor introduction, with all its constraints, is the only way to gain access to the community. This circumstance requires the ethnographer to begin in the hole, overcompensating to prove himself or herself worthy and to earn the community's trust and respect. This predicament forces the ethnographer to disassociate diplomatically from the intermediary once inside but act honorably and acknowledge the debt owed to that first contact.

Selecting an integral and powerful member of the community is useful, but establishing independence in the field is also important to avoid prematurely cutting off other lines of communication. For example, in a library study, a close link with the power brokers was instrumental in my gaining access to the organization but was almost lethal to data collection. My alliance with a power broker created the perception that I was a spy or another power broker sitting on the wrong side of the fence. In attempting to understand how the subordinate and disenfranchised group functioned in the bowels of the library, I found myself persona non grata. Tremendous effort was necessary for me to prove myself an impartial or at least nonjudgmental witness and shed the guilt I had acquired by association.

Once in the community, specific methods and techniques will guide the ethnographer in the process of data collection and analysis. The remainder of this chapter will discuss each of these techniques in turn.

PARTICIPANT OBSERVATION

Participant observation characterizes most ethnographic research and is crucial to effective fieldwork. Participant observation combines participation in the lives of the people under study with maintenance of a professional distance that allows adequate observation and recording of data. Powdermaker's *Stranger and Friend* (1966) vividly depicts this delicate role. Participant observation is immersion in a culture. Ideally, the ethnographer lives and works in the community for 6 months to 1 year or more learning the language and seeing patterns of behavior over time. Long-term residence helps the researcher internalize the basic beliefs, fears, hopes, and expectations of the people under study. The simple, ritualistic behaviors of going to the market or to the well for water teach how people use their time and space and how they determine what is precious, sacred, and profane.

The process may seem unsystematic; in the beginning, it is somewhat uncontrolled and haphazard. Even in the early stages of fieldwork, however, the ethnographer searches out experiences and events as they come to attention. Participant observation sets the stage for more refined techniques—including projective techniques and questionnaires—and becomes more refined itself as the fieldworker understands more and more about the culture. Ideas and behaviors that were only a blur on entering the community take on a sharper focus. Participant observation can also help clarify the results of more refined instruments by providing a baseline of meaning and a way to reenter the field to explore the context for those (often unexpected) results.

When I lived in Israel, I saw small and large patterns of behavior that repeated themselves almost endlessly. Passengers took the presence of bombs on the buses in stride; the soldiers and their ever-present Uzis (submachine guns) became part of the woodwork. The cycle of planting and harvesting on the kibbutz was marked by sweat and blood, strained muscles, and aching joints—and by seasonal holidays and festivals.

Every day had its pattern. Kibbutzniks and the other students and volunteers in my group woke up at 4:00 a.m. and walked down to the *hader ochel,* or dining room, for a small snack and then began work in the fields at 4:30 or 5:00 a.m. Every morning (except for the Saturday sabbath), we bundled up with our kibbutz army jackets to ward off the morning chill on the way to the fields. We stripped away the jackets after half an hour or so of work, when the sun began to heat the fresh morning air. We built up quite an appetite for breakfast by 8:00 or 9:00 a.m., but breakfast slipped by and we were back in the fields before we were rested. When we picked peaches, the heat and the itchy peach fuzz drove us crazy. Lunch and a shower were a saving grace. The break after lunch to read, socialize, or visit the children at the nursery was a pleasure to savor each day. With luck, another crisis task to work on would relieve the monotony of the morning's job—even though such a distraction meant equally demanding manual labor. When dinnertime finally arrived, we trooped back to the hader ochel for an unvaried dinner: fish on Sundays, chicken on Fridays, and a mixture of the two in between. Even the raising of children followed a cycle on the kibbutz. Pregnant mothers who had grown up and worked together had their babies at approximately the same age, and they later congregated with their strollers around the day care facility.

In the old city of Jerusalem, other rituals took place—by the Wailing Wall and blocks away in the Arab shops. Hasidic Jews (*Lubavitch rebbes*) who wore long hair locks (*payahs*), broad black fur hats (*fadorahs*), and long black coats and worshiped by the Wailing Wall invited me to live and study with them for a short time to share their inner secrets and way of life. Similarly, Arab merchants who befriended me while I lived in Jerusalem often closed down their shops in the middle of a busy business day to have tea with me, bringing out all their silver-plated trappings, special glasses filled with tea leaves and 2 inches of undissolved sugar on the bottom, and ceremonial rugs. They enjoyed a sense of timelessness I will never forget.

All these patterns were recognizable over time, and detailed observations were possible only by living and working in these communities. I had to prepare the fields, plant the seeds, irrigate the soil, and pick the fruits in the kibbutz; study with the Hasidim; and bargain every day with the Arab merchants to understand and record these very different ways of life. Working with people, day in and day out, for long periods of time is what gives ethnographic research its validity and vitality.

Given time, people forget their "company" behavior and fall back into familiar patterns of behavior. Ethnographic research in one's own culture may not require as much time to reach this point as ethnographic work in a foreign culture: Language and customs are familiar, and the researcher is already an insider in many respects. Sometimes a familiar setting is too familiar, however, and the researcher takes events for granted, leaving important data unnoticed and unrecorded.

In applied settings, participant observation is often noncontinuous and spread out over an extended time. For example, in two ethnographic studies, one of dropouts and the other of gifted children, I visited the programs for only a few weeks every couple of months during a 3-year period. The visits were intensive and included classroom observation, nonstop informal interviews, occasional substitute teaching, interaction with community members, and the use of various other research techniques, including long-distance phone calls, dinner with students' families, and time spent hanging out in the hallways and parking lot with students cutting classes.

Participant observation requires close, long-term contact with the people under study. In the two cases discussed previously, the time period was 3 years. Often, contract research budgets or time schedules do not allow long periods of study—continuous or noncontinuous. In these situations, the researcher can apply ethnographic techniques to the study but cannot conduct an ethnography. Similarly, observation without participation in other people's lives may involve ethnographic methods but is not ethnography. Nonparticipant observation may take such forms as watching a school basketball game as part of data collection. Applying ethnographic techniques and nonparticipant observation are acceptable forms of research, but labeling the research method correctly is important.

The process may seem complicated, but a good ethnographer starts with the basics. Participant observation begins with the first question—even as simple a question as *Apho ha bait shemush?* (Where is the bathroom?). Finding the bathroom or kerosene for a heater can help the researcher understand a community's geography and resources. Slowly but surely, the questions become more refined as the researcher learns what questions to ask and how to ask them.

In any case, the acquisition of ethnographic knowledge and understanding is a cyclical process. It begins with a panoramic view of the community, closes in to a microscopic focus on details, and then pans out to the larger picture again—but this time with new insight into minute details. The focus narrows and broadens repeatedly as the fieldworker searches for breadth and depth of observation. Only by both penetrating the depth and skimming the surface can the ethnographer portray the cultural landscape in detail rich enough for others to comprehend and appreciate.

INTERVIEWING

The interview is the ethnographer's most important data gathering technique. Interviews explain and put into a larger context what the ethnographer sees and experiences. They require verbal interaction, and language is the commodity of discourse. Words and expressions have different values in various cultures. People exchange these verbal commodities to communicate. The ethnographer quickly learns to savor the informant's every word for its cultural or subcultural connotations as well as for its denotative meaning. General interview types include structured, semistructured, informal, and retrospective interviews. Although in practice these types overlap and blend, this chapter will artificially isolate interview types, strategies, and questions for purposes of description and discussion. Each interviewing approach has a role to play in soliciting information. The ethnographer, however, should be clear on the pros and cons of each interview type in data collection and analysis before employing these approaches in the field (for alternative approaches to classifying interviews, see Denzin, 1978; Goetz & LeCompte, 1984; Patton, 1980; for additional discussion about interviewing techniques, see Bogdan & Biklen, 1982; Hammersley & Atkinson, 1983; Taylor & Bogdan, 1984; Werner & Schoepfle, 1987a).

Formally structured and semistructured interviews are verbal approximations of a questionnaire with explicit research goals. These interviews generally serve comparative and representative purposes—comparing responses and putting them in the context of common group beliefs and themes. The fieldworker can use a structured interview at any time in the study. For example, a list of questions about the educational background of the teachers in a school under study is useful in securing comparative baseline data about the teachers' qualifications and experience. Asking those questions can also be a nonthreatening icebreaker. At the beginning stages of a study, however, structured interviews tend to shape responses to conform to the researcher's conception of how the world works. These interviews are therefore most useful at the middle and end stages of a study for the collection of data about a specific question or hypothesis. A structured or semistructured interview is most valuable when the fieldworker comprehends the fundamentals of a community from the "insider's" perspective. At this point, questions are more likely to conform to the native's perception of reality than to the researcher's.

Informal interviews are the most common in ethnographic work. They seem to be casual conversations, but whereas structured interviews have an explicit agenda, informal interviews have a specific but implicit research agenda. The researcher uses informal approaches to discover the categories of meaning in a culture. Informal interviews are useful throughout an ethnographic study in discovering what people think and how one person's perceptions compare with another's. Such comparisons help identify shared values in the community—values that inform behavior. Informal interviews are also useful in establishing and maintaining a healthy rapport.

Informal interviews seem to be the easiest to conduct. They do not involve any specific types or order of questions, and they can progress much as a conversation does, following the turns of the participant's or the questioner's interests. These interviews, however, are probably the most difficult to conduct appropriately and productively. Issues of ethics and control emerge from every informal interview. How does the fieldworker establish and maintain a natural situation while attempting to learn about another person's life in a relatively systematic fashion? How can a completely open form, ripe for discovery, balance with an implicitly shaped structure designed to explore specific issues and concerns? Finally, when is the time to take advantage of a golden opportunity and when is it best not to pry further? Done well, informal interviewing feels like natural dialogue but answers the fieldworker's often unasked questions.

Informal interviews should be user-friendly. In other words, they should be transparent to the participant after a short period of time. An informal interview is different from a conversation, but it typically merges with one, forming a mixture of conversation and embedded questions. The questions typically emerge from the conversation. In some cases, they are serendipitous and result from comments by the participant. In most cases, the ethnographer has a series of questions to ask the participant and will wait for the most appropriate time to ask them during the conversation (if possible).

Informal interviews offer the most natural situations or formats for data collection and analysis. Unfortunately, some degree of contamination is always present. However skillful the interviewer, certain questions will impose an artificiality. An experienced interviewer, however, learns how to begin with nonthreatening questions deeply embedded in conversation before posing highly personal and potentially threatening questions and to develop a healthy rapport before introducing sensitive topics. Sensitivity to timing and to the participant's tone is critical in interviewing—informal or otherwise. The chance to ask a gang member about illegal activities might be lost if during the interview that individual receives a phone call from another gang member warning about an unidentified informer in the community. That moment, however, might be the best time to ask about informants and the pressures of community life. An ethnographer must learn to be attentive to a person's shifts in tone because these changes are important cues to attitudes and feelings. An elderly woman's shift from soft, eloquent speech to frightened, quivering whispers when she mentions the death of her spouse is a cue that the questioner should proceed delicately. She may want to discuss the topic as part of a cathartic experience or may feel pressured into divulging inner secrets. These situations are never easy. A sensitive and experienced ethnographer, however, will be able to differentiate between the two situations and to act appropriately. The researcher will make mistakes along the way. (See Fetterman, 1983, and Chapter 7 for a discussion of the ethical hazards ethnographers face in the field.)

The chance to exploit a vulnerable individual to secure invaluable data may be tempting. In fact, it may be a rare opportunity to explore an individual's innermost secrets. Beyond the obvious ethical considerations, however, the cost of exploiting an individual is too high, and the ethnographer must either wait for another opportunity to come along or create one. One benefit of spending long periods of time at a site is that other, more propitious opportunities usually come along. Oversensitivity, however, can paralyze an ethnographer, placing unnecessary obstacles in the way of data collection and analysis.

A multitude of significant nonthreatening questions can elicit the information the fieldworker seeks and create many golden moments in which to ask questions naturally as part of the general flow of conversation. Planning and executing properly placed questions, while maintaining a flexible format, is the essence of good ethnography, ensuring the quality of the data and maintaining the participant's right to privacy.

Retrospective interviews can be structured, semistructured, or informal. The ethnographer uses retrospective interviews to reconstruct the past, asking informants to recall personal historical information. This type of interview does not elicit the most accurate data. People forget or filter past events. In some cases, retrospective interviews are the only way to gather information about the past. In situations in which the ethnographer already has an accurate understanding of the historical facts, a retrospective interview provides useful information about the individual. The manner in which individuals shape the past highlights their values and reveals the configuration of their worldviews.

Ethnographers use interviews to help classify and organize an individual's perception of reality. All interviews share some generic kinds of questions. The most common types are survey or grand tour, detail or specific, and open-ended or closed-ended questions. Survey questions help identify significant topics to explore. Specific and detailed questions explore these topics in more detail. They determine similarities and differences in the ways people view the world. Open-ended and closed-ended questions help the ethnographer discover and confirm the participant's experiences and perceptions.

Survey or Grand Tour Question

A survey question—or what Spradley and McCurdy (1972) call a grand tour question—is designed to elicit a broad picture of the participant or native's world and to map the cultural terrain. Survey questions help define the boundaries of a study and plan wise use of resources. The participant's overview of the physical setting, universe of activities, and thoughts helps to focus and direct the investigation.

In a study about a university, a typical survey question would be the following: Could you show me around the university? In responding to this question, the individual would teach about the different academic and business departments, the hospital, the church or synagogue or both, the student union, the library, the fraternities, and so on. The quality of a grand tour question determines its usefulness. The narrower the survey question, the narrower the response and, in turn, the resulting overview of a culture. At the same time, the scope of the study determines the scope at which a survey question is useful. For example, if the study includes an entire university, then the previous tour question would be a good survey question. If the study comprises the whole of American culture, asking an individual to show the ethnographer around verges on the ridiculous; in limited settings, this approach can be highly misleading.

In my study of a university library, I asked one individual to show me around. I took a tour of familiar grounds: the reference desk, the electronic and hard-copy catalog files, special collections, and various graduate and undergraduate collections. I also saw the behind-the-scenes places: administrative offices, basement rooms of uncataloged books, cataloging rooms, rooms filled with computer hardware and software, and other unfamiliar locations. This information helped me to refine the scope of my study; at the same time, it provided a context within which to frame my investigation. This grand tour helped me understand how books and people flow through the library system. Parts of the library operated like a production line; others followed the model of a community of medieval scholars and illuminators. Once I had a good grasp of how much I did not know, I developed somewhat narrower survey questions. For example, I realized that I did not know what librarians did on a daily basis—so I asked.

Survey questions led to information that allowed me to construct a basic map of the place, develop a model of how it worked, and isolate preliminary topics that enabled me to use my time more efficiently and effectively. Such information also stimulated a barrage of specific, detailed questions, followed by more survey questions, and leading once more to detailed questions—until I had constructed a satisfactory conceptual framework.

Ethnographic research requires the fieldworker to move back and forth between survey and specific questions. Focusing in on one segment of a person's activities or worldview prematurely may drain all the ethnographer's resources before the investigation is half done. The fieldworker must maintain a delicate balance of questions throughout the study; in general, however, survey questions should predominate in the early stages of fieldwork and more specific questions in the middle and final stages.

Specific Questions

Once survey questions reveal a category of some significance to both fieldworker and native, specific questions about that category become most useful. The difference between a survey question and a specific or detailed question depends largely on context. The question, "What do librarians do?," is a grand tour question in a library study, but it would be a specific question in a university study.

In my library study, specific questions focused on the differences among divisions within the library and among types of librarians in each division—for example, between the curator in public services and the original cataloger in technical services. More refined specific questions concerned the differences between two members of the same division and department, such as those between an original cataloger and a copy cataloger in the catalog department.

Specific questions probe further into an established category of meaning or activity. Whereas survey questions shape and inform a global understanding, specific questions refine and expand that understanding.

Structural and attribute questions—subcategories of specific questions—are often the most appropriate approach to this level of inquiry. Structural and attribute questions are useful to the ethnographer in organizing an understanding of the native's view. For example, a series of structural questions in the library study included the following: "What are the major parts of the library?" "How is this place organized?" and "What kinds of departments or divisions exist in the library?" The responses to these questions provided the insider's perspective on the library's structure. I learned about three major divisions: public services, technical services, and administrative services. Probing further, I elicited a detailed description of the departments within these divisions. Following up with another structural question, I asked, "What types of librarians work in each of these divisions?" Participants explained that catalogers and conservationists work in separate departments within one division, and curators work in a completely different division. For greater generalizability, I compared perceptions of several individuals to identify similarities and differences in perspective resulting from power, status, and role differences. I also called and visited other research libraries to learn whether this structural pattern was typical of research universities throughout the country. (Telephone and written questionnaires are useful tools for determining how representative the particular patterns are within an organization and across organizations.) Structural questions provide the similarities that exist across the conceptual spectrum—in the native's head. (See Spradley & McCurdy, 1972, for additional information about the construction of taxonomic definitions.)

Attribute questions—questions about the characteristics of a role or a structural element—ferret out the differences between conceptual categories. Typically, the interview will juxtapose structural with attribute questions. Information from a structural question might suggest a question about the differences between various newly identified categories. For example, after learning about the various divisions and departments that constitute a research library, I could logically ask about the differences between them using the following attribute question: "What is the difference between librarians who work in technical services and librarians who work in public services?" In addition to learning the functional differences between these two positions, I learned much about perceived discrepancies in status between catalogers who work in the "bowels of the library"—in near sweatshop conditions, unseen by the rest of the university—and curators, who work with students, staff, and faculty in plush, air-conditioned, carpeted offices with plenty of space and light. To discover more about each division and department, I followed this response with the following structural question: "What are the departments in technical services?" Librarians eagerly taught me about the various departments in that division, including acquisitions, cataloging, serials, binding and finishing, and conservation. The following attribute question was then useful in clarifying my understanding of the library's organization: "What is the difference between acquisitions and cataloging?"[1] The response to this question gave me a clearer idea about the production flow of the books in this system. (See Spradley & McCurdy, 1972, for a discussion about componential analysis.)

Structural and attribute questions derive from a cognitive theory (symbolic interactionism) about how the world works (Blumer, 1969). Clearly, however, these question types are valuable in almost any theoretical approach because they help to organize the fieldworker's perception of how others define reality.

Open-Ended or Closed-Ended Questions

Ethnographers use both open-ended and closed-ended questions to pursue fieldwork. An open-ended question allows participants to interpret it.

For example, in studying an emergency room, I asked a regular emergency room nurse the following question: "How do you like working with the helicopter nurses?" This question elicited a long and detailed explanation about how aloof she thought they were and how unfair it was that the helicopter nurses did not pitch in during the busy periods. She said she could list five or six activities that emergency room and helicopter nurses did together during the week, but she said these activities were all superficial.

This response opened new doors to my study. I followed up with questions to helicopter nurses, who indicated that they did wait around a great deal of the time waiting for a call to rush to the helicopter. They explained that they could not pitch in during regular emergency room busy periods because they might be called away at any time, and leaving in the middle of a task would be unfair to both the regular nurses and the patients. Thus, an open-ended question helped to illuminate the conflicting world-views these two sets of nurses held about the same emergency room experience—information that a closed-ended question, such as "How many times do you interact with the helicopter nurses each week?" might not have elicited.

Closed-ended questions are useful in trying to quantify behavior patterns. For example, asking both sets of nurses how many times they interact with each other in a week would be a useful test of varying perceptions of reality and a means of documenting the frequency of that particular behavior pattern. Differing responses would also be a useful cue to probe further about the quality of that interaction.

Ethnographers typically ask more open-ended questions during discovery phases of their research and more closed-ended questions during confirmational periods. The most important question to avoid is the stand-alone vague question. Asking regular nurses whether they work with helicopter nurses frequently—without defining frequently—is useful to neither the researcher nor the participant.

Interviewing Protocols and Strategies

A protocol exists for all interviews—the product of the interviewer's and the participant's personalities and moods, the formality or informality of the setting, the stage of research, and an assortment of other conditions.

The first element common to every protocol is the ethnographer's respect for the culture of the group under study. In an interview or any other interaction, ethnographers try to be sensitive to the group's cultural norms. This sensitivity manifests itself in apparel, language, and behavior. Wearing expensive designer clothes to conduct an informal interview with a disenfranchised and impoverished high school student is as insensitive and inappropriate as wearing cutoff jeans and a T-shirt to conduct an interview with a chief executive officer. Inadvertent improprieties or faux pas will occur, and people will generally forgive them. A consistent disregard or lack of concern for the group's basic cultural values, however, will severely impede research progress.

Second, an overarching guide in all interviews is respect for the person. An individual does the fieldworker a favor by giving up time to answer questions. Thus, the interview is not an excuse to interrogate an individual or criticize cultural practices. It is an opportunity to learn from the interviewee. Furthermore, the individual's time is precious: Both the industrial executive and the school janitor have work to do, and the ethnographer should plan initial interviews, whether formal or informal, around their work obligations and schedules. Later, the fieldworker becomes an integral part of the work. Even greater sensitivity to the nuances of timing are essential at this point, however. The observant ethnographer responds to signals from the interviewee. Repeated glances at a watch are usually a clear signal that the time is up. Glazed eyes, a puzzled look, or an impatient scowl is an interviewee's way of letting the questioner know that something is wrong: The individual is bored, lost, or insulted. Common errors involve spending too much time talking and not enough time listening, failing to make questions clear, and making an inadvertently insensitive comment. The ethnographer must listen to the language of the interviewees. In one fashion or another, they are always communicating.

In formal settings, such as a school district, a highly formalized, ritualistic protocol is necessary to gain access and interview students and teachers. Soliciting and securing permission may involve an introductory meeting with various stakeholders (including the superintendent and principal) to exchange pleasantries, a formal explanation of the research project (including submission of the proposed research), letters of permission, and periodic formal exchanges, including notice of the study's termination. Similarly, structured interviews require a more structured protocol of introductions, permission, instructions, formal cues to mark major changes in the interview, closure, and possible follow-up communications.

Informal interviews require the same initial protocol. The researcher, however, casually and implicitly communicates permission, instructions, cues, closure, and follow-up signals. Pleasantries and icebreakers are important in both informal and formally structured interviews, but they differ in the degree of subtlety each interview type requires. Sensitivity to the appropriate protocol can enhance the interviewer's effectiveness.

Strategies or techniques can also enhance the quality of an interview. The most effective strategy is, paradoxically, no strategy. Being natural is much more convincing than any performance. Acting like an adolescent does not win the confidence of adolescents, it only makes them suspicious. Similarly, acting like the consummate lawyer is useless during an interview with lawyers for obvious reasons. First, ethnographic training emphasizes honesty in fieldwork, including interviews. Deceptive games have no place in the interview setting or elsewhere. Second, in any data gathering interview, the objective is to learn from the interviewee and not to impress the person with how much the questioner already knows about the area. Third, even a consummate actor is bound to slip during a lengthy interview and thus undermine all credibility. Being natural is the best protection.

More experienced ethnographers learn when it is appropriate or possible to test their knowledge of the system by breaking a minor cultural norm, such as sitting in someone else's chair during an official meeting to test status, hierarchy, and grouping patterns. This knowledge development strategy, however, requires a great deal of experience and a very healthy rapport, usually the product of much time spent with the group under study. Being cavalier about even minor cultural norms can be quite costly in hurt feelings, damaged rapport, and severely distorted lines of communication—all resulting in bad data.

A degree of manipulation takes place in any interview. The interviewer is trying to learn something about an individual's life—not everything about it. Achieving this goal requires some conscious or subconscious shaping of the verbal exchange—through either explicit or implicit cues borrowed from the cues in natural conversation. For example, to borrow a strategy from courtroom proceedings, asking the same question in several different ways within one session checks both the interviewer's understanding of the response and the individual's sincerity—that is, whether the answer is what the person believes or what he or she wants the ethnographer to hear (or thinks the ethnographer wants to hear). This strategy usually provides the ethnographer with a slightly modified, refined understanding of the initial response. Often, repeated questions or variations of the same question draw responses that shed a completely new light on the topic. The interviewer should scatter these types of questions throughout the interview. One right after another, repeated questions can be insulting and fruitless. Some interviews reach the point of diminishing returns more quickly than others. The interviewer must recognize when to linger and when to move on.

A similar strategy involves asking for repetition of the participant's questions. A person's questions are as informative as his or her answers. In repeating a question, the interviewee provides a broader perspective on the topic and on relevant concerns. Similarly, the interviewer can ask the interviewee to repeat or clarify an answer when the tone or manner of the answer triggers some doubt about the completeness of the response. This approach is effective in stimulating discussion with an interviewee who responds to inquiries with only terse, efficient replies.

Of the hundreds of useful interviewing strategies, the most successful place the interviewee at ease, acknowledge the value of the information, and reinforce continued communication. Many books about interviewing also emphasize control. In formal structured and semistructured interviews, maintaining control of the direction of the interview is useful to ensure that the interview produces the target information in the short time allotted. The ethnographer wants the interviewee to be in control much of the time, however. The "how" of communication is as instructive as the "what." A person's manner, emphasis, and presentation can teach much about that person's perception of time, organization of thoughts, and feelings about interpersonal relationships. Taking charge of most interviews and maintaining control of them can sacrifice too many data. The skillful ethnographer learns when to let the interviewee ramble and when to shape or direct the information flow—a decision generally shaped by the stage of research or inquiry. In exploratory work, letting the participant control the communication flow is most useful. Focused periods of formal hypothesis testing require that the ethnographer maintain greater control.

Silence is also a valuable interview strategy. Learning how to tolerate the empty space between question and reply is difficult for many Americans. The fieldworker, however, learns not to routinely jump in and clarify a question whenever silence falls. The best approach is to let the participant think about the question and digest it for a while before responding. After the participant has apparently finished discussing a topic, a brief pause can bring out more information or an important qualification to the information. The burden of silence falls on both parties. An experienced ethnographer learns how to use silence in a skillful fashion—to encourage interviewees to speak but not to make them feel uncomfortable or threatened. Such strategies, and those described in the following sections, will ensure a more natural and useful flow of communication, minimizing role playing, various other contaminating factors, and nonproductive time.

Key Actor or Informant Interviewing

Some people are more articulate and culturally sensitive than others. These individuals make excellent key actors or informants. *Informant* is the traditional anthropological term. I use the term *key actor*, however, to describe this individual to avoid both the stigma of the term informant and its historical roots.[2] In the social group under study, this individual is one of many actors and may not be a central or even an indispensable community member. This individual, however, becomes a key actor in the theater of ethnographic research and plays a pivotal role, linking the fieldworker and the community.

Key actors can provide detailed historical data, knowledge about contemporary interpersonal relationships (including conflicts), and a wealth of information about the nuances of everyday life. Although the ethnographer tries to speak with as many people as possible, time is always a factor. Therefore, anthropologists have traditionally relied most heavily on one or two individuals in the group.

Typically, the key actor will find many of the ethnographer's questions obvious or stupid. The fieldworker is asking about basic features of the culture—elementary knowledge to the key actor. Such naive questions, however, often lead to global explanations of how a culture works. Such responses point out the difference between the key actor and a respondent. The key actor generally answers questions in a comprehensive, albeit meandering fashion. A respondent answers a question specifically, without explanations about the larger picture and conversational tangents with all their richness and texture. Interviewing a respondent is usually a more efficient data collection strategy, but it is also less revealing and potentially less valid than discussions with a key actor.

Key actors require careful selection. They are rarely perfect representatives of the group. They are usually, however, members of the mainstream—otherwise, they would not have access to up-to-date cultural information. Key actors may be cultural brokers straddling two cultures, such as the dropouts in my study who had one foot in the school and one in the streets. This position may give them a special vantage point and objectivity about their culture. They may also be informal or formal leaders in the community. Key actors come from all walks of life and all socioeconomic and age groups.

Key actors are excellent sources of information and important sounding boards for ethnographers. In site visits during my study of dropouts, I often went first to one of my key actors for updating on the latest events and to sound out my newest ideas about cultural practices and beliefs. Rerun, a student in the Brooklyn program for dropouts, often invited me to his home for dinner or to listen to records. He and his grandmother told me stories about the neighborhood—how it used to be and how dangerous it had become. He also showed me around the community so that I would learn "how the other half lived." His hangouts included fronts for drug transactions and hotels for pimping, prostitution, and an assortment of related activities. This community knowledge was invaluable from his perspective, and he was quite willing to share it with me. This same information helped me to understand the contextual background of the school program. Rerun also gave me an insight into the school ethos by focusing on the importance of role modeling in the school. He told me about a new teacher in the program who broke all the rules concerning appropriate apparel and tried to teach them about "liberating merchandise" using a "five-fingered discount." He said the students rebelled. They went right to the director to complain about her. "They were here to learn," he explained. They had already seen what that type of instruction had done for them in public schools and in the streets. The new teacher had broken such basic cultural norms in the program that the student population had her removed. I cross-checked this information with the director and various other parties. Although the director was reluctant to discuss it, he confirmed Rerun's story and provided information that other sources had withheld because of its politically embarrassing nature.

James was a long-term janitor in the Detroit drop-out program. He grew up in the local community with many of the students and was extraordinarily perceptive about the differences between the serious and less serious students in the program as well as between the serious and less serious teachers. I asked him whether he thought the students were obeying the new restrictions against smoking, wearing hats in the building, and wearing sneakers. He said,

> You can tell from the butts on the floor that they are still smokin', no matter what dey tell yah. I know, cause I gotta sweep 'em up. . . . It's mostly the new ones, don't yah know, like Kirk, and Dyan, Tina. You can catch em olmost any ol' time, I seen 'em during class in the hallways, here [in the cafeteria], and afta-hours [in the cafeteria].

He provided empirical evidence to support his observations—a pile of cigarette butts he had swept up while we were talking.

In a study of a gifted and talented education program, my most insightful and helpful key actor was a school district supervisor. He told me about the politics of the school district and how to avoid the turf disputes during my study. He drove me around the community to teach me how to identify each of the major neighborhoods and pointed out corresponding socioeconomic differences that proved to have an important impact on the study (Fetterman, 1986f, 1988a). He also described the cyclical nature of the charges of elitism raised against the program by certain community members and a former school board member. He confided that his son (who was eligible to enter the program) had decided not to enter. This information opened new doors to my perception of peer pressure in that community. A key actor who provides concrete descriptions is usually more helpful than one who becomes tangled in abstractions. In another study, one key actor was another anthropologist working in an educational program. At first, his help was invaluable. As the study proceeded, however, his concrete descriptions and periodic symbolic interpretations gave way to full-blown theoretical propositions about the entire social system. Eventually, we both recognized that we were losing sight of the program and the individuals in the study. Highly trained, formally educated key actors can be instrumental in research, but the fieldworker should solicit their contributions with great care, emphasizing the concrete and tying abstractions down to reality.

Key actors can help synthesize the fieldworker's observations. In a university department under study, I observed a series of faculty meetings in which no one could make a decision about any issue for months. I had come to expect some ambiguity, argument, and dissension, but I could not make sense of this prolonged period of instability; these faculty members were usually much more decisive. I shared my description of the faculty as a ship adrift, sailing aimlessly without a rudder, with a key actor (an emeritus faculty member from that department). He helped me to make sense of what I had observed and experienced by providing a wider context. He explained that I was experiencing the "interregnum." The former chair had been deposed, and the department had a leadership vacuum. Without this information, I could not have completed my picture of departmental interactions.

Key actors and ethnographers must share a bond of trust. Respect on both sides is earned slowly. The ethnographers must take the time to search out and spend time with these articulate individuals. The fieldworker learns to depend on the key actor's information—particularly as cross-checks with other sources prove it to be accurate and revealing. Sometimes, key actors are initially selected simply because they and the ethnographer have personality similarities or mutual interests. Ethnographers establish long-term relationships with key actors who continually provide reliable and insightful information. Key actors can be extremely effective and efficient sources of data and analysis.

At the same time, the ethnographer must judge the key actor's information cautiously. Overreliance on a key actor can be dangerous. Every study requires multiple sources. In addition, care is necessary to ensure that key actors do not simply provide answers they think the fieldworker wants to hear. The ethnographer can check answers rather easily but must stay on guard against such distortion and contamination. Another more subtle problem occurs when a key actor begins to adopt the ethnographer's theoretical and conceptual framework. The key actor may inadvertently begin to describe the culture in terms of this a priori construct, undermining the fieldwork and distorting the emic or insider's perspective (for further discussion of the role of key informants, see Dobbert, 1982; Ellen, 1984; Freilick, 1970; Goetz & LeCompte, 1984; Pelto, 1970; Spradley, 1979; Taylor & Bogdan, 1984).

Life Histories and Expressive Autobiographical Interviews

Key actors often provide ethnographers with rich, detailed autobiographical descriptions. These life histories are usually quite personal; the individual is usually not completely representative of the group. How a key actor weaves a personal story, however, tells much about the fabric of the social group. Personal description provides an integrated picture of the target culture.

Many of these oral histories are verifiable with additional work. In some instances, however, the life history may not be verifiable or even factually accurate. In these cases, the life history is still invaluable because the record captures an individual's perception of the past, providing a unique look at how the key actor thinks and how personal and cultural values shape his or her perception of the past. Together with observation and interviewing, taking life histories allows the ethnographer to assemble a massive amount of perceptual data with which to generate and answer basic cultural questions about the social group.

My fieldwork on the kibbutz yielded several rich and rewarding life histories. Many of the older kibbutzniks were concentration camp survivors. Their stories about pre-concentration camp life, survival in the camps, and their experiences up to the present were riveting and powerful. One survivor, Abraham, described his family in his youth, the schools he attended in Germany, the positions he held, and the gradual change in atmosphere as the Nazi party gained power. He told me how he lost half his family in the ghetto before the remainder even reached the camps. His stories about the strategies for survival in the camp were frightening. He survived the camp because the Nazis let him live as long as he went down into the pits filled with dead bodies to pick the gold teeth from the corpses. He remembered the cold day the Nazis lined him up next to his brother and arbitrarily shot his brother and left him alive. We even discussed how some prisoners from a once high-status social class still felt superior to others in the camps. Svie was another Holocaust survivor. He described a young man who rebelled in the camps. Seeing a rifle standing by the corner of the building where they were to be gassed, the young man ran naked and shivering from the line to grab the rifle. He aimed it at the guards and pulled the trigger, but it was empty: The guards had tricked him. They told the young man that others would have to pay for his disobedience and then shot 30 men, women, and children in front of him before herding him back in line to be gassed. The stories of physical and psychological terror the survivors had experienced in the past—and the guilt that many still felt simply for surviving when so many had died—were overwhelming. These stories were valuable not only as historical records but also as keys to helping me understand the behavior, moods, fears, and values they displayed each day at work on the kibbutz.

The dropout program study also provided rich life histories. Many of the students shared their lives with me in great detail. One young woman told me that her mother repeatedly stole her boyfriends from her and left her out in the cold at night to fend for herself; a young man described seeing his best friend shoot at the police and seeing his friend shot in the neck by them in return. These graphic life histories helped to explain how these individuals viewed the world—why some had dropped out of school, why they were periodically late for the new program, and why they needed so many counselors in the program. Furthermore, the life history of a secretary in one of the drop-out programs—a perfect picture of a white, middle-class young woman—explained why she was in conflict with predominantly black lower-socioeconomic-class children.

The life history approach is usually rewarding for both key actor and ethnographer. It is exceedingly time-consuming, however. Approximations of this approach, including expressive autobiographical interviewing, are particularly valuable contributions to a study with resource limitations and time constraints. In many cases, an abbreviated or focused life history is sufficient. An expressive autobiographical interview or case history combines a structured interview with a chronological autobiography. The autobiography focuses on social, educational, or career development. Rather than learning about the participant's life in a holistic fashion, the ethnographer learns in some depth about one facet of the participant's life. The depth of perspective these techniques provide is invaluable in putting the pieces of the puzzle together. This approach is most likely to pay off by generating useful insights into a participant's view of the world and relating those insights to the specific topic of study in a short period of time (Spindler & Spindler, 1970, p. 293).

LISTS AND FORMS

A number of techniques can stimulate the interviewer's recall and organize the data. During a semistructured interview, a protocol or topical checklist can be useful. Printed or unobtrusively displayed on a portable computer screen, these lists usually contain the major topics and questions that the ethnographer plans to cover during the interview. A checklist can be both a reminder and a mechanism to guide the interview when a more efficient approach is desirable. Similarly, after some experience in the field, the fieldworker can develop forms that facilitate data capture. For example, I developed a classroom observation form for myself and other fieldworkers in the dropout study. It consisted simply of spaces for the date, site, observer, teacher, and class subject at the top of the page, with the rest of the page divided into three sections: preclass observation, description of classroom instruction, and postclass description. The form was simple to follow and complete. It was also open-ended, allowing the observer to record any events. The only explicit structure I imposed on the form—and thus on the observation—was a categorization of the types of activities before, during, and after class, including mention of which students came to class early or remained after class and specifically what they were doing. Documenting the mood that teachers and students brought to the class through interviews and observations often helped explain classroom behavior, particularly during periods of extracurricular activities such as election campaign periods and big games.

Checklists and forms help to organize and discipline data collection and analysis. Their construction should rely on some knowledge from the field to ensure their appropriateness and usefulness. Checklists and forms also require consistent use, thus allowing the fieldworker to compare, for example, various dropouts' views about a new rule or regulation in their system. Such lists and forms, however, are not cast in stone; new topics emerge that merit exploration. New conceptualizations arise, and different forms are necessary for collection and analysis of the relevant data. Thus, the researcher must continually modify old lists and forms and develop new ones throughout the study.

QUESTIONNAIRES

Structured interviews are close approximations of questionnaires. Questionnaires are perhaps the most formal and rigid form of exchange in the interviewing spectrum—the logical extension of an increasingly structured interview. Questionnaires are qualitatively different from interviews, however, because of the distance between the researcher and the respondent. Interviews have an interactive nature that questionnaires lack. In filling out a questionnaire, the respondent completes the researcher's form without any verbal exchange or clarification. Knowing whether the researcher and the respondent are on the same wavelength, sharing common assumptions and understandings about the questions, is difficult—perhaps impossible.

Misinterpretations and misrepresentations are common with questionnaires. Many people present an idealized image on questionnaires, answering as they think they should to conform to a certain image. The researcher has no control over this type of response and no interpersonal cues to guide the interpretation of responses. Other problems include bias in the questions and a poor return rate. Population samples derived from telephone books exclude the large number of people with unlisted numbers, without telephones, or in the process of moving. Random-digit dialing represents an improvement, but it still misses the latter two groups. Similarly, using car registrations to devise a sample will miss people who do not own or register cars. Ignoring these often discrete populations will systematically affect the data and the interpretation of the responses.

Despite these caveats, questionnaires are an excellent way to tackle questions dealing with representativeness. They are the only realistic way of taking the pulses of hundreds or thousands of people. Anthropologists usually develop questionnaires to explore a specific concern after they have a good grasp of how the larger pieces of the puzzle fit together. The questionnaire is a product of the ethnographer's knowledge about the system, and the researcher can adapt it to a specific topic or set of concerns. Ethnographers also use existing questionnaires to test hypotheses about specific conceptions and behaviors. The ethnographer, however, must establish the relevance of a particular questionnaire to the target culture or subculture before administering it. In developing a brief questionnaire for two studies, I used my knowledge of the culture, reflected in cultural terms and expressions, the way questions were phrased, and the content of the questions. A pilot phase was necessary to eliminate all types of errors, including vague and misleading questions, inappropriate response categories, excessive size, and poor print quality. I also had to send out three waves of questionnaires to improve the response rate. Additional statistical work was necessary to account for sample bias in the returns and to resolve a number of other problems. I then compared the results of these questionnaires and tests with my descriptive findings. The descriptive findings were useful in explaining the questionnaire results, and the questionnaire results provided some insight into the wide range of certain attitudes. Questionnaires have their place in ethnographic research: They are an efficient means of large-scale data collection. Despite all precautions, however, the methodological problems associated with questionnaire use—including the distance between questioner and respondent—weaken its credibility as a primary data collection technique. (See Fowler, 1988, for an excellent presentation of survey research methods; see Hagburg, 1970, about the validity of questionnaire data; and see Groves & Kahn, 1979, and Lavrakas, 1987, concerning telephone surveys.)

PROJECTIVE TECHNIQUES

Projective techniques are also useful in ethnographic research. Projective techniques supplement and enhance fieldwork; they do not replace it. These techniques elicit cultural and often psychological information from group members. Typically, the ethnographer holds an item up and asks the participant what it is. The anthropologist may have an idea about what the item represents, but that idea is less important than the participant's perception. The participant's responses usually reveal individual needs, fears, inclinations, and general worldview.

The Rorschach ink blot tests are a classic projective technique. The psychologist or psychiatrist holds up a series of ink blots and asks the patient to interpret them. The clinician makes a diagnosis based on the information the patient provides. Anthropologists have used the Rorschach, the Thematic Apperception Test, and a variety of other psychological tests to investigate specific hypotheses (Pelto, 1970; Spindler & Spindler, 1958). The use of projective techniques in fieldwork presents some difficulties, however. First, the researcher needs special training and experience in administering the tests and in interpreting the responses. Second, these tests are culturally biased—relevant primarily to the culture that produced them. Unless the researcher adapts the tests—or the interpretation of them—to the culture under study, the interpretations may be inappropriate and the findings misleading.

Many anthropologists adapt these tests to fit the local context. Others simply use classic projective techniques to elicit a response from a participant and then use judgment and intuition (based on an understanding of the community) to interpret the response appropriately. Still other anthropologists invent projective techniques to suit their purposes. I frequently use pictures and slides as projective techniques. In the drop-out study, I showed students pictures of their neighborhood and asked them to explain the pictures so that I could learn how they mapped out their community. I also showed them slides of each other to elicit responses. A slide showing the program's director, of whom I had heard only high praise, drew shouts of "Idi Amin." The students' response had revealed another facet of their feelings for the director: They loved and respected him, but they also hated him for being a taskmaster, enforcing all the school rules. I needed to investigate this response further through follow-up interviews and various cross-checks. The slide, however, provided the first glimmer into this aspect of the student-director relationship.

Simply taking a picture can be a projective technique. I take pictures in almost all my studies. How an individual responds to the camera as I focus the lens often characterizes an individual. Shy, bold, or sexy postures are all telling.

A casual discussion about movies, television shows, the police, or almost any topic can be a projective technique for a skillful and attentive ethnographer. As a teacher and a researcher in an inner-city high school, I used dreams as projective techniques. I asked students about their dreams and the dreams of others and then asked them what they meant. Their dreams of being cornered in a classroom and trapped in the principal's office closely paralleled their feelings of being imprisoned in school. (In exchange for their openness, I often provided a classic Freudian or a pragmatic Adlerian interpretation of their dreams. They enjoyed these interpretations primarily for their entertainment value.)

Projective techniques, however revealing, rarely stand alone. The researcher needs to set these techniques in a larger research context to understand elicited responses completely. Projective techniques can be cues to lead to further inquiry or one of several sources of information to support an ongoing hypothesis. Only the ethnographer's imagination limits the number of possible projective techniques. The fieldworker, however, should use only those tests that can be relevant to the local group and the study.

ADDITIONAL ELICITING DEVICES

A variety of other tools elicit the insider's classification and categorization of a target culture. Ethnographers ask participants to rank-order people in their community to understand the various social hierarchies. The semantic differential technique (Osgood, 1964) elicits an insider's rating of certain concepts. For example, a respondent is asked to rate rock music on a five-point Likert-type scale (excellent, good, neutral, bad, and awful). (The fieldworker and native share the same definitions of these ratings.) The native or participant is then asked to rate a variety of other concepts. The fieldworker can compare this individual's ratings with those of others in the community to produce a picture of how the group thinks about certain issues. The fieldworker can thus identify patterns and statistical outliers or anomalies. Cognitive mapping is also useful in eliciting the insider's perspective. Asking a student to map out his or her walk to school with various landmarks—for example, a route that identifies gang territories by block—provides an insight into how that individual views the world.

These techniques, like projective techniques, require some baseline knowledge of the community before their design and use. Additional work is necessary after administering these devices to comprehend fully what the responses mean. These techniques can achieve the same findings that interviews with structural and attribute questions yield—the insider's perception of reality.

UNOBTRUSIVE MEASURES

This chapter began by stating that ethnographers are human instruments, dependent on all their senses for data collection and analysis. Most ethnographic methods are interactive: They involve dealing with people. The ethnographer attempts to be as unobtrusive as possible to minimize the effects on the participant's behavior. Data collection techniques—except for questionnaires—fundamentally depend on that human interaction.

A variety of other measures, however, do not require human interaction and can supplement interactive methods of data collection and analysis. These methods require only that the ethnographer keep eyes and ears open. Ranging from outcroppings to folktales, these unobtrusive measures draw social and cultural inferences from physical evidence (Webb, Campbell, Schwartz, & Sechrest, 1966).

Outcroppings

Outcropping is a geological term referring to a portion of the bedrock that is visible on the surface—in other words, something that sticks out.

Outcroppings in inner-city ethnographic research include skyscrapers, burned-out buildings, graffiti, the smell of urine on city streets, yards littered with garbage, a Rolls-Royce, and a syringe in the schoolyard. The researcher can quickly estimate the relative wealth or poverty of an area from these outcroppings. Initial inferences are possible without any human interaction. Such cues by themselves, however, can be misleading. A house with all the modern conveniences and luxuries imaginable can signal wealth or financial overextension verging on bankruptcy. The researcher must place each outcropping in a larger context. A broken syringe can have several meanings, depending on whether it lies on the floor of a doctor's office or in an elementary schoolyard late at night. On the walls of an inner-city school, the absence of graffiti is as important as its presence.

One young woman student wore a rabbit-fur coat, skin-tight and revealing dresses, high heels, and layers of jewelry to class. Her clothes suggested a possible identification with pimps and prostitution. (Her active involvement in this lucrative profession was later confirmed by the director and, in an unsolicited and coincidental meeting, her probation officer.)

Kirk and Dee wore special emblems on their jackets that clearly stated their gang affiliation. I eventually learned that only one of them maintained a gang affiliation. The young man was wearing his brother's jacket.

Changes in a physical setting over time can also be revealing. For example, an increase in the number of burned-out and empty buildings on a block indicates a decaying neighborhood. Conversely, an increase in the number of remodeled and revitalized houses may be indicative of gentrification, in which wealthy investors take over the neighborhood. A classroom with current and complex projects prominently displayed on the walls suggests classroom activity and learning. Academic and athletic trophies are measures of performance in these areas and tokens of school pride. The fieldworker must assess this abundant information with care but should not ignore it or take it for granted.

Written and Electronic Information

In literate societies, written documents are one of the most valuable and timesaving forms of data collection. In studies of office life, I have found past reports, memoranda, and personnel and payroll records to be invaluable. Mission statements and annual reports provide the organization's purpose or stated purpose and indicate the image that the organization wishes to present to the outside world. Internal evaluation reports indicate areas of concern. Budgets tell a great deal about organizational values. Electronic communications and databases not only teach the researcher about the current status of an organization but also allow the computer-literate ethnographer to play "what-if" games with the data. For example, the ethnographer can exchange or substitute figures on a departmental spreadsheet to determine the effects of different assumptions and conditions. Electronic mail is often less inhibited than general correspondence and thus quite revealing about office interrelationships, turf, and various power struggles.

School records tell where the school has been, is, and plans to be in the future (or at least what the party line says are the school goals). Lesson plans, homework assignments, essays, and report cards (or the absence of any of these outcroppings) are revealing sources of information about students, teachers, parents, and administrators. Minutes from board of education and faculty meetings provide useful retrospective information. The fieldworker needs permission to gain access to these types of records, particularly the more sensitive data. The number of written records stored in old file cabinets or files on floppy disks and mainframes can be staggering, however. Proper use of this type of information can save the ethnographer years of work.

Proxemics and Kinesics

Proxemics and kinesics were discussed briefly in Chapter 2 in an explanation of the difference between micro- and macrolevel studies. Briefly, *proxemics* is the analysis of socially defined distance between people, and *kinesics* focuses on body language (Birdwhistell, 1970; Hall, 1974). Students who remain physically distant from their teachers may feel a tenuous relationship with them. In American culture, a salesperson speaking about a product who is 2 inches away from a prospective buyer's face has probably intruded on the buyer's sense of private space. A skillful use of such intrusion may overwhelm the customer and make the sale, but it is more likely to turn the customer off. Seating arrangements at meetings have social meaning. At an advisory panel meeting in the drop-out study, the power brokers trying to control the meeting sat at one end of the table, and their opponents established their own territory at the other end. Shifts in the seating arrangements during the meeting evidenced shifts in power and allegiance. The relative status and social distance between interviewer and interviewee are often evident in the physical distance between them during the interview. The interviewer who sits behind a desk throughout an interview is sending a different message from the interviewer who comes around the desk and sits alongside the interviewee. This seating arrangement may indicate how the interviewer feels about dominant and subordinate relationships or it may indicate the interviewer's level of comfort or unease in this type of stressful social situation. The fieldworker should record these observations, and—as with many of the techniques in this chapter—put them in a larger context for interpretation and cross-check the findings with other data.

Sensitivity to body language can also be instrumental in ethnographic research. A clenched fist, a student's head on a desk, a condescending superior's facial expression, a scowl, a blush, a student sitting at the edge of a chair with eyes fixed on the lecturer, and many other physical statements provide useful information to the observant fieldworker. In context, this information can generate hypotheses, partially confirm suspicions, and add another layer of understanding to fieldwork.

Folktales

Folktales are important to both literate and nonliterate societies. They crystallize an ethos or a way of being. Cultures often use folktales to transmit critical cultural values and lessons from one generation to the next. Folktales usually draw on familiar surroundings and on figures relevant to the local setting, but the stories themselves are facades. Beneath the thin veneer is another layer of meaning. This inner layer reveals the stories' underlying values. Stories provide ethnographers with an insight into the secular and the sacred and the intellectual and the emotional life of a people.

Biblical myths and folktales are used today in Israel to reinforce certain national values. Similarly, folktales about George Washington and his father's cherry tree are used to instill certain values in young children and adults in the United States. Listening to community folktales about dropouts, for example, provides evidence about how community members perceive dropouts. Student folktales about gangs may indicate their attitude toward gangs and their involvement with them.

Folktales are present in all settings. In a study of a hospital pharmacy, I found folktales to be quite informative about the culture. One of the most serious financial concerns in a hospital pharmacy is loss of revenue. I identified a big hole in the operation by listening to and following up on information derived from folktales. Listening to the medical records employees swap "war" stories about patient records told me that certain departments had been hoarding records for years. Other stories depicted great fights between medical departments for possession of certain sensitive (and financially valuable) records. I learned about ancient records found behind filing cabinets in the medical records department. This story was told over and over again to comfort employees: They had an antiquated, labor-intensive, manual system and had been unsuccessful in efforts to cajole management into adding staff or computerizing the system. The folktales reinforced their subcultural belief that they were an oppressed or neglected cog in a big, expensive machine. Their stories had more than a grain of truth. The antiquated manual system was responsible for a significant loss of revenue. The departments did not have enough employees to process the records (converting medications administered to patients into charges) or to handle all the work; therefore, some records just piled up until it was too late to charge the patient. Administrators used this same folktale as a scapegoating mechanism to blame the department for their losses by reinforcing an image of ineptitude. This folktale led to important insights into the organization's maladaptive behavior.

Folktales in the emergency room about heroic efforts to save patients maintained the morale of the doctors and nurses during especially difficult times. Folktales also shaped behavior in the administrative sections of the emergency room. One of the first tales I heard when talking with some of the emergency room staff was about the supervisor. The emergency room supervisor had a reputation for reviewing every travel reimbursement to nurses and physicians. I knew the supervisor very well, and I knew that he did not have time to review any of these financial concerns—he relegated them to an assistant, who looked at only a fraction of the expenses incurred in the emergency room. The folktale about the supervisor's tight controls, however, sent a symbolic message throughout the system that management controls its resources by paying close attention to detail. This folktale had an effect on petty concerns such as travel reimbursements and on basic medical practices in the emergency room. Once again, the perception of reality is more important than so-called objective reality in shaping behavior. (See Fetterman, 1986g, for additional details about these studies, with a focus on administrative and financial concerns.)

All the methods and techniques discussed in this chapter are used together in ethnographic research. They reinforce one another. Like concepts, methods and techniques guide the ethnographer through the maze of human existence. Discovery and understanding are at the heart of this endeavor. Chapter 4 explores a wide range of useful devices that make the ethnographer's expedition through time and space more productive and pleasant.

NOTES

1. I decided to focus on the catalog department at this point and asked the following structural question: "What types of librarians work in this department?" Two specific

types of librarians became the focus of discussion: original and copy catalogers. A natural attribute question in this context was the following: "What is the difference between an original and copy cataloger?" This question drew an emotionally charged discussion about how radically different were their daily lives, how different the required training was for each position, and how different were the intellectual efforts of each type of librarian. I learned how the copy catalogers used existing catalog information to do their job, whereas the original catalogers must decipher the book first and then follow a labyrinth of codified rules and regulations to complete the task. After a little probing, the original catalogers informed me how little they thought management appreciated this difference. This feeling was based on their new "production" standards—the number of books they were expected to process in a day. Some original catalogers explained that they felt they were working in a dying profession. They explained that every new book is already cataloged by the Library of Congress for the copy catalogers and that they are cataloging only the old books from before the Library of Congress "took over." Many original catalogers believe they are simply working themselves out of a job. This type of cultural knowledge is invaluable in trying to understand the inner workings of a complex organization, including its stresses and strains.

2. The term informant has its roots in anthropological work conducted in colonial settings, specifically in African nations formerly within the British empire (Evans-Pritchard, 1940, 1951; Pi-Sunyer & Salzmann, 1978, pp. 451-453). The term also conjures up images of clandestine activities that are incompatible with an ethnographic approach.

4

Gearing Up:
Ethnographic Equipment

On smooth surfaces the staff helps
maintain an easy rhythm to my walk
and gives me something to lean on
when I stop to stand and stare.

—Colin Fletcher

Notepads, computers, tape recorders, and cameras—all the tools of ethnography—are merely extensions of the human instrument—aids to memory, capacity, and vision. These useful devices, however, can facilitate the ethnographic mission by capturing the rich detail and flavor of the ethnographic experience and then helping to organize and analyze the data. This chapter surveys ethnographic equipment, including simple paper and pen, tape recorders, cameras, videocassette recorders, high-tech computers, database software, Internet search engines, and web pages. Proper equipment can make the ethnographer's sojourn in an alien culture more pleasant, safe, productive, and rewarding.

PEN AND PAPER

The most common tools ethnographers use are pen and paper. With these tools, the fieldworker records notes from interviews during or after each session, sketches the physical layout of an area, traces an organizational chart, and outlines informal social networks. Notepads can hold initial impressions, detailed conversations, and preliminary analyses. Most academics have had a great deal of experience with this simple tool by taking extensive notes in classes. This skill is easily transferred to the field. Pen and paper have several advantages: ease of use, minimal expense, and unobtrusiveness. The drawbacks are obvious: The fieldworker cannot record every word and nuance in a social situation, has difficulty maintaining eye contact with other participants while writing, and must expend a great deal of effort to record data that are legible and organized.

TAPE RECORDER

Ethnographers attempt to immerse themselves in the field, working with people rather than devices. Tools that free the ethnographer from manual recording are welcome. Tape recorders allow the ethnographer to engage in lengthy informal and semistructured interviews without the distraction of manual recording devices. Tape recorders effectively capture long verbatim quotations, essential to good fieldwork, while the ethnographer maintains a natural conversational flow. The tapes can be analyzed over and over again. In all cases, however, the fieldworker should use the tape recorder judiciously and with consent.

Tape recorders can inhibit individuals from speaking freely during interviews. Individuals may fear reprisals because their voice is identifiable. The ethnographer can minimize these concerns by emphasizing the confidentiality of data. Sometimes, slowly easing into the use of tape recorders avoids unnecessary tension. I usually begin with pen and pad, and when the conversation picks up speed I ask if I can switch to the tape recorder—simply because I cannot write fast enough to catch every word. I also stop the recorder whenever I touch on a topic that the interviewee thinks is too sensitive to have on tape. A quick response to these requests highlights the ethnographer's sensitivity and integrity, strengthening the bond between ethnographer and participant.

Tape recorders are useful icebreakers. On several occasions, I recorded students' songs on the tape recorder and played the music back for them before asking about the school being studied. During group interviews, I typically ask students to pass the tape recorder around and introduce themselves on it as though they were celebrities. This approach often makes them eager to participate in the discussion and usually makes them comfortable with the machine. It also enables me to accurately identify each participant's words long after leaving the field.

Tape recorders do, however, have some hidden costs. Transcribing tapes to printable text is an extremely time-consuming and tedious task. Listening to the tape takes as much time as making the original recording; for many researchers, hours of interview data require hours of listening. Transcribing the tape adds another dimension to the concept of time consumption. Typically, the fieldworker edits the tapes, transcribing only the most important sections. A carefully selected professional transcriber can remove this burden if funds are available. The transcriber must be familiar with the language, dialect, and slang of the people on the tape; must know to note—not gloss over—inaudible sections; and must be able to transcribe in a way that is value-neutral or context-relevant. One of my first transcribers was very familiar with black English vernacular—a must for the tapes I needed transcribed. She was black and from a low- to middle-income family. Unfortunately, she believed that black English vernacular was degrading and did not want lower-socioeconomic-class black students represented in a way she thought degrading. Consequently, she smoothed out their conversation, making sure it resembled white middle-class speech. Having conducted all the interviews myself and knowing the students fairly well, I recognized the problem at once. I explained why I needed verbatim transcriptions. My transcriber, however, continued to eliminate the student's expletives in her transcriptions. The role of values, even in this facet of ethnographic investigation, proved to be a critical link in the chain of research.

CAMERAS

Cameras have a special role in ethnographic research. They can be a "can opener" to provide rapid entry into the community or classroom (Collier, 1967; Fetterman, 1980). They are a known commodity to most industrialized and to many nonindustrialized nations. I use cameras to help establish an immediate familiarity with people. Cameras can create pictures useful in projective techniques or can be projective tools themselves. They are most useful, however, in documenting field observations.

The camera enables the ethnographer to create a photographic record of specific behaviors. I documented changes in student style of dress as one manifestation of an attitudinal change during tenure in the drop-out program. Cameras can capture moments of understanding between friends or contrast the joy of a young boy running in and out of the cold water pouring out of an open hydrant on a hot sticky day in the city with a backdrop of poverty, dilapidated tenements, and littered streets. During the drop-out study, I documented tremendous physical contrasts—evidencing considerable economic differences—between Manhattan and Brooklyn, New York: The shining United Nations building, Saint Patricks' Cathedral, Carnegie Hall, and Bloomingdales juxtaposed with burned-out buildings, blocks of rubble, graffiti, garbage, broken glass, drug hangouts, small street corner businesses, and tiny Pentecostal churches. As Collier (1967) explained,

> Photography is a legitimate abstracting process in observation. It is one of the first steps in evidence refinement that turns raw circumstances into data that are manageable in research analysis. Photographs are precise records of material reality. They are also documents that can be filed and cross-filed as can verbal statements. Photographic evidence can be endlessly duplicated, enlarged or reduced in visual dimension, and fitted into many schemes of diagrams, and by scientific reading, into many statistical designs. (p. 5)

I documented the decay of an inner-city neighborhood by photographing the buildings during every site visit during a 3-year period. These photographs vividly displayed the growing problem of arson. This documentation is particularly useful when comparing notes with coworkers in the field. In this study, another investigator and I disagreed about our descriptions of the neighborhood. The other observer thought the area was in reasonable condition; I thought it was severely decayed and worsening. My colleague, however, typically took a cab directly to the school, without spending time in the neighborhood. I made a point of spending a great deal of time in the neighborhood taking photographs and learning about the environment before even entering the school. As evidence, my photographs were compelling. They were labeled, cross-referenced with map locations, and tabulated according to severity of decay and decay over time. The disagreement was easily resolved.

Photographs can aid memory. During analysis and writing periods, photographs and slides can bring a rush of detail that the fieldworker might not remember otherwise. By capturing cultural scenes and episodes at the beginning of a study—before the ethnographer has a grasp of the situation—pictures allow the ethnographer to interpret events retroactively, offering a rare second chance. Also, the camera often captures details that the human eye has missed. Although the camera is an extension of the subjective eye, it can be a more objective observer and less dependent on the fieldworker's biases and expectations. A photographic record provides information that the fieldworker may not have noticed at the time. Photographs and slides are also excellent educational tools both in the classroom and in a sponsor's plush conference room. In class, slides can vividly show students a world they might never see in any other context and are useful in demonstrating specific methodological and theoretical points. Slides can also be useful in educating research sponsors. Graphic representations of behaviors and locations can be illuminating and compelling. My slides of the inner-city—the context of a drop-out program—had a powerful impact on the funding agency that was far beyond the impact of test scores and descriptions. The sponsors were able to appreciate with greater clarity and understanding the difficulties the schools had to surmount to continue operating. They could then appreciate the gains and losses on student test scores in these schools.

The standard complement of photographic equipment in the field includes a 35-mm single lens reflex (SLR) camera, a lens, and rolls of film. A variety of excellent 35-mm cameras are available. A portrait lens is adequate for most purposes in the field. A telephoto lens (for distant objects) and a macrolens (for a close-up view) can also be useful. I use a small lightweight automatic camera that has a relatively quiet shutter and a small built-in zoom lens, which is relatively unobtrusive in social situations. High-speed film (400 to 1600 ASA) eliminates the need for an obtrusive flash in most cases. Unfortunately, enlargements of high-speed film will be grainy. Lower-speed films are best if enlargements are needed. I also use a digital camera to facilitate transfer to the Internet. Several choices are available: hand-held cameras, such as Casio's LCD camera, or non-hand-held digital cameras that only plug into my computer, such as Connectix's QuickCam camera.

The fieldworker should select photographic equipment to suit personal taste and individual competence or expertise. Hundreds of useful accessories are available ranging from tripod and flash to developing equipment. The aim, however, is to choose equipment that answers the needs of fieldwork and not to become lost in technological sophistication. Given careful treatment, a modern automatic or SLR camera should last a lifetime. Technological developments will continue to advance photography considerably but will not necessarily make a camera obsolete for fieldwork.

The use of the camera in fieldwork requires permission. Some people are uncomfortable having their picture taken. Many groups I worked with in Israel had strong religious reasons for not wanting their picture taken, including a fear of losing their souls. The issue involves individual privacy: The ethnographer must enter the lives of people on their terms but may not invade individual privacy. Photography is often an intrusion. People are usually self-conscious about their picture and concerned about how and where it will be seen. An individual's verbal permission is usually sufficient to take a picture. Written permission, however, is necessary to publish or display that picture in a public forum. Even with verbal and written permission in hand, the ethnographer must exercise judgment in choosing an appropriate display and suitable forum.

Using the camera can cause problems. Inappropriate use can annoy and irritate people, undermining rapport and degrading the quality of the data. Cameras can also distort reality. A skillful photographer uses angles and shadows to exaggerate the size of a building or shape the expression on a person's face. The same techniques can present a distorted picture of an individual's behavior. For example, much horseplay mimics physical aggression. Snapping the shutter at the right moment and angle might suggest real violent behavior when there truly is none. Taken out of context, pictures, like words, can be misleading. The fieldworker must be as careful in photographing human behavior as in recording an interviewee's comments and concerns. Time in the field is necessary before photographs and slides become meaningful and before the ethnographer can make an accurate and systematic record of the norm. Photographs are useful in gaining an understanding of a cultural norm, but do not stand alone. The fieldworker needs to learn the rules and values of a culture to complete the picture. (Intentional distortions, such as inappropriate cropping or alterations in negatives, evidence gross disregard for the truth. See Becker [1979] for an excellent discussion of photography and threats to validity. See also the visual anthropology journals, *Studies in Visual Communication* and *Visual Anthropology Review.*)

VIDEOTAPE

Videotape recordings are extremely useful in microethnographic studies. Ethnographers usually have a fraction of a second to reflect on a person's gesture, posture, or gait. Videotape provides the observer with the ability to stop time. The ethnographer can tape a class and watch it over and over, each time finding new layers of meaning, nonverbal signals among participants. Over time, visual and verbal patterns of communication may become clear when seen repeatedly and in stop action.

Several years ago, a colleague and I conducted a study of two high school history classes using videotape. One class was predominantly lower-socioeconomic-class minority students; the other class, with the same teacher, was primarily white, upper-middle-class students. We observed a clear difference in teaching styles and classroom atmospheres. Documenting these differences was the problem. The tapes helped us make sense of what was happening in the two classes. Using the videotapes, we were able to identify specific behaviors the teacher used to solicit information or to silence the students. The videotapes also helped identify subtle teacher cues to the students.

Videotape equipment is essential to any microethnographic research. Gatekeeping procedures (Erickson, 1976) and the politics of the classroom (McDermott, 1974) are elements of complex social situations that the fieldworker can capture on tape. The fieldworker, however, must weigh the value of the equipment and the time required to use it against the value of the information it will capture. Many ethnographic studies simply do not need a fine-grained picture of social reality. In addition, the actual expense of using videotape equipment—including camera, videotapes, and the videotape machine—is not trivial. This equipment is also notably obtrusive. Even after spending time in the history classes with and without the equipment, we still saw mugging or posing for the camera.

The most significant hazard in using videotape equipment is the risk of tunnel vision. Ideally, the ethnographer has studied the social group long enough to know where to focus. The ethnographer may need months to develop a reasonably clear conception of specific behaviors before deciding to focus on them for a time. The videotape can focus on a certain type of behavior to the exclusion of almost all else in the classroom. Thus, the ethnographer may arrive at a very good understanding of a specific educational mechanism but achieve little understanding of its real role in the classroom. In addition, the technology aggravates the problem—inherent in all research—of seeing what one wants to see. During the history class study, I videotaped students in the back of the class who were sending notes to each other or sleeping and one student in the front of the class who was horsing around. My colleague compared his written notes with my videotape and said he documented as many students in the same class who were highly attentive and actively participating in class. This cross-checking and other techniques, such as asking students and teachers to review the tapes, helped to refine and validate our work. This experience, however, provided a useful reminder of how easily we could become wrapped up in videotaping and lose sight of the big picture—or even the small picture. Experience teaches ways to mitigate many of these problems—for example, by sweeping across the classroom periodically to avoid unintentional overfocusing.

CINEMA

The use of cinema or movies in ethnographic research is rare. In ethnography, movies primarily present a finished picture of a cultural group; they are not tools the researcher uses to compose this picture. Cost and expertise as a filmmaker and editor are additional factors associated with the limited use of cinema.

Ethnographic films have rigorous requirements, ranging from actual time sequencing to authenticity of the event recorded. Heider (1976) produced a scale of "ethnographicness" to judge ethnographic films. This attribute dimension includes such variables as ethnographic basis, relations to print, whole acts, whole bodies, explanation of distortions, technical competence, narration fit, ethnographic presence, contextualization, whole people, distortions in filmmaking (time and continuity), inadvertent distortion of behavior, and intentional distortion of behavior (pp. 46-117). Most ethnographers agree that ethnographic films still supplement, rather than replace, a written text or ethnography. (For additional information about the use of cameras, videotapes, and filmmaking in ethnographic research, see Bellman & Jules-Rosette, 1977; Collier, 1967; Erickson & Wilson, 1982; Hockings, 1975; the Society for Visual Anthropology also maintains up-to-date information about this topic at http://custwww.xensei.com/docued/sva/.)

COMPUTERS: LAPTOP AND DESKTOP

The laptop computer is a significant improvement over pen and notepad. Laptop computers are truly portable computers for use in the office, on a plane, and in the field. I often use one in lieu of pen and paper during interviews. In technologically sophisticated settings, they are rarely obtrusive or distracting if the fieldworker introduces the device casually and with consideration for the person and the situation. Laptop computers save time better spent thinking and analyzing. Laptops eliminate the need to type up raw data—the interview notes—every day. The fieldworker enters these data into the computer only once—during or immediately after an interview. These notes can be expanded and revised with ease. The files can transfer from the laptop to a desktop computer or mainframe with a floppy, zip, jazz, or other high-storage capacity disk or external drive; appropriate software; infrared beam; high-speed modem, or all of these. Increasingly, laptops serve as the primary or only computer because they are as fast and have as much storage capacity as most desktop computers.

Laptops also provide the ethnographer with an opportunity to interact with participants at critical moments of analysis. Ethnographers can share and revise notes, spreadsheets, and graphs with participants on the spot. I routinely ask participants to review my notes and memoranda as a way to improve the accuracy of my observations and to sensitize me to their concerns. Graphic representations of behavior frequencies, funds, or size of subcultures within an organization can open the eyes of both the ethnographer and the participant. Laptops enable participants to provide immediate feedback and play with the variables to see the possibilities—for example, removing one group from the picture, substituting one for another, or merging groups or funds together. The ethnographer learns much about the participant's values from this type of thoughtful play with the data. The types of combination that are acceptable to the participant provide a useful insight into the participant's views.

The laptop computer is not a panacea, but it is a real time-saver and is particularly useful in contract research. Ethnographers who conduct multisite research can carry all their programs to the sites and send files back to the home base by using a modem to link with a home computer. Laptops also greatly facilitate communication from the field to the research center through interactive electronic-mail systems. I often attach my field notes to e-mail letters while in the field. This allows me to back up my work by sending it to myself and to share my notes with colleagues on a multisite project. When sharing field notes, I code my data, use pseudonyms, and limit distribution of my notes to protect key actors and ensure confidentiality. These files can then merge with other field data, forming a highly organized (dated and cross-referenced), cumulative record of the fieldwork.

Laptops have drawbacks of course, as does all equipment. Machines fail, and backing up data is critical and easy to do with zip, jazz, and swappable hard drives. Batteries discharge, and it is wise to purchase an extra one for long interviews or plane trips. Surge protectors are required when using a desktop computer, but many colleagues forget that the same safety precaution should be applied to laptops to protect the machine and the data. I always carry a small one with me. I was thankful that I checked with electric bulletin board colleagues before venturing forth to work in South Africa. My colleagues reminded me that my surge protector would work only for 110-voltage lines and that the standard in Africa was 220 V. It was a valuable reminder: I might have "fried" the surge protector while thinking I was protecting my computer. Another drawback is that the clatter of the keyboard can sometimes be distracting and obtrusive. In most cases, however, a brief desensitization will make people feel comfortable with the equipment after the fieldworker takes the time to acquaint them with it. In fact, the laptop can be an icebreaker, helping to develop a strong rapport with people and at the same time inuring them to its presence. If they are introduced into the situation carefully, laptops or any piece of equipment can greatly facilitate ethnographic work (Figure 4.1).

BOX 4.1

I used a PowerBook computer in preparing and revising this book, writing drafts on airplanes, at meetings, at relative's houses, and outdoors. I use this machine at home, in the field, in the office, and wherever I travel. The power and portability of the unit allow me to continue working in settings and during times that are typically not conducive to productive effort.

Many of the points and issues raised in the laptop discussion also apply to desktop computers. Many researchers prefer to upload or send their files from a laptop to a desktop computer with more storage capacity for extensive manipulation.

The combination of coprocessor, memory, and hard disk represents a critical combination of computer components enabling the manipulation of large data sets. The speed of coprocessors, the amount of computer memory, and the size of hard and external drives rise exponentially across time. Although the rapid pace of development makes computers technologically obsolete the moment you purchase them, they are not functionally obsolete. I have conducted a number of projects and written a couple of books on technologically obsolete machines that were still capable of handling word processing, spreadsheet calculations, database management, and telecommunications. Eventually, however, the hardware limitations associated with an older unit (particularly as they relate to surfing the net or supporting newer software programs) detract from your ability to do your work effectively. It is important to upgrade and update your computers and software periodically to avoid the need for an expensive transition and translation process from one system to another. The appropriate configuration of computer components allows the ethnographer the freedom to compare and contrast a huge number of variables with ease.

THE INTERNET

The Internet is one of the most powerful resources available to ethnographers. It can be used to conduct searches about a topic, analyze census

Figure 4.1. Example of a Laptop Computer: An Apple PowerBook
SOURCE: Courtesy of Apple Computer, Inc.

data, conduct interviews by "chatting" or videoconferencing, share notes and pictures about a research site, debate issues with colleagues on listservs and in on-line journals, and download useful data collection and analysis software. A brief review of web resources, including software available on the web, and the addresses of useful websites will start you on your exploration of this rich resource (see the list of URLs—Uniform Resource Locator—provided at the end of this chapter). The Internet refers to a worldwide network of computers talking a language known as TCP/IP. Tens of millions of persons in the United States alone work or play with computers that are connected to this network, and worldwide the number must exceed 100,000,000. To most users (including ethnographers and other researchers and scholars), however, the Internet appears as e-mail and the World Wide Web (WWW). The former is probably familiar to anyone reading this book; estimates are that the number of e-mail letters sent in the United States first exceeded the number of paper postal items in 1995. The WWW, which was virtually unheard of in 1993, now occupies a prominent place in world popular culture; the once obscure symbol http:// is now ubiquitous. The WWW is a standardized method of transferring files (text, graphics, and audio) across the Internet and can result in attractive, vivid, and engaging presentations (known as web pages) to persons connecting to the Internet via web browsers (Netscape and Microsoft Internet Explorer currently being the most popular).

It seems likely that e-mail, web browsing, and, as the speed of telecommunications inevitably increases, videoconferencing will constitute the core of Internet use for researchers and scholars in the near future.[1] One thing is certain: The evolution of cheap, worldwide telecommunications via networked computers will make available to researchers an astounding array of resources to aid them in their work. Exactly what these resources will be is not clear.

When this book first appeared in 1989, it concluded here. The pencil is as old as Asyrian cuneiform tablets. The camera and telephone are more than 100 years old. The WWW, however, did not exist in 1989. I cannot guess what advances will occur by the time this chapter is printed. I will attempt to keep you up-to-date by maintaining a website with information about and links to resources for ethnographers. Please visit the sites at http://www-leland.stanford.edu/~davidf/ethnography.html and http://www-leland.stanford.edu/~davidf/webresources.html.

Search, Reference, and
Directory Assistance Pages

Search engines are computer programs designed to find and list specified sites and resources on the web. Some of the most powerful search engines include AltaVista, Excite, HOTBOT, and Yahoo. An ethnographer can retrieve such various and relevant information as pictures of a potential site, maps, literature on a given topic or site, demographic information about a location, historical data, and even music and sounds associated with a region.

A simple search on the word ethnography in AltaVista will yield a list of more than 8,000 hypertext links. As users quickly discover, the vastness of the Internet as a data source is also its weakness. Sifting through information data dumps can be overwhelming. Typically, search engines organize information from the most relevant to the least relevant items. More refined search engines are being developed, but be prepared to invest some time sifting the wheat from the chaff, as in any library literature search.

Reference pages, such as Xplore (Figure 4.2) and the New York Times Navigator, link you to an extraordinary array of information sources, ranging from the Library of Congress, the White House, and the Smithsonian Institution, to the complete works of William Shakespeare. They also provide links to practical references—for example, currency convert-

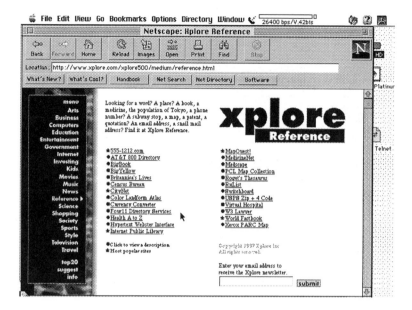

Figure 4.2. Xplore Reference Page
SOURCE: Reproduced with permission from Jeff Rich, President, Xplore, Inc.

ers and free medical resources such as MedicineNet. The Federal Web Locator facilitates searches of agencies and departments (particularly valuable for action and advocacy ethnographers).

LookupUSA is one of the most powerful directory assistance pages on the net, providing the capability to search information on approximately one billion households and businesses. It allows ethnographers to find individual telephone numbers to personal homes, which is particularly useful when following a lead with an illegibly written or unknown address. Most lists of addresses for follow-up studies conducted months or years after the initial research are hopelessly outdated. LookupUSA allows you find the address and telephone number of individuals in the telephone book. MapsOnUs (Figure 4.3) as well as MapQuest can be used to provide maps of street addresses if you already have the address.

This resource saves a lot of time and energy, but it illustrates another side to the power of the Internet: invasiveness. Although it provides only public information, it makes such information much more accessible, dramatically transforming its potential value. It should not be abused; permission to follow up and interview individuals is still required. Zip2 and Four11 are other valuable address directories.

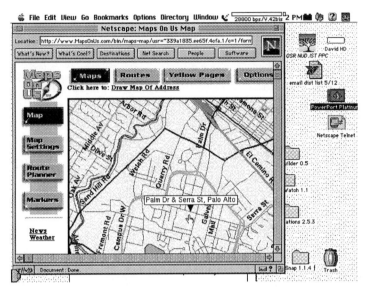

Figure 4.3. MapsOnUs Map
SOURCE: Reproduced with permission from Richard Trapp.

Ethnographers can also search the globe to view specific locations from the comfort of their own homes. Cameras posted throughout the world are linked to the Internet. For example, Live Cam Pictures World Wide provides a list of locations from Antarctica to the United Kingdom. These views are useful as a preview before entering a site, a view while temporarily away from a site, a mnemonic device to bring memories back to life while writing, a tool to view change over time, and an inexpensive means to reminisce about a past fieldwork site and stimulate thoughts for future work. EarthCam, Peeping Tom, and Bill's Random Camera sites offer a list of additional locations.

DATA COLLECTION SOFTWARE

MicNotePad (Figure 4.4) is a piece of freeware or publicly available software that turns a PowerBook into a tape recorder and facilitates

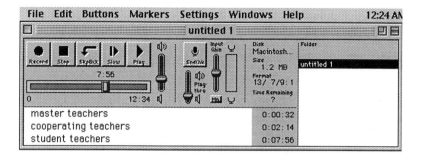

Figure 4.4. Screen Snapshot of MicNotePad
SOURCE: Reproduced with permission from Nirvana Research, MicNotePad
at http://moof.com/nirvana

transcription. After gaining the participant's or key actor's permission, as I do with a tape recorder, I use it in the field to record interviews unobtrusively and to play back sections to make sure the speaker agreed that the statement accurately reflected his or her thoughts. In addition, this software allows the ethnographer to mark key points or phrases in the interview, allowing quick information retrieval, as well as identification of patterns in the conversation or interview. This software also facilitates transcription because it allows you to skip back and replay a sentence (until the entire passage has been typed), slow down the virtual "tape," and, with embedded commands, control the recording while typing on a word processor. Mic-NotePad is available at the University of Kent's Centre for Social Anthropology and Computing software server.

There are various commercial dictation software programs, such as Power Secretary by Dragon or IBM Voice Type Gold, that can greatly facilitate traditional transcription. These programs allow you to dictate text directly into wordprocessing and spreadsheet files. The highest quality dictation software can distinguish between words such as "to" and "two" in a sentence based on the context of the word. In addition, high quality programs have active-noise canceling headset microphones. However, most of these programs require a fast co-processor, intensive memory, and almost ideal conditions, since they do not always filter out background noise.

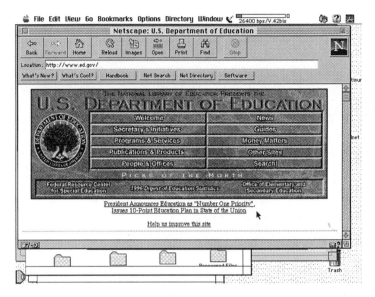

Figure 4.5. U.S. Department of Education Web Page

Web Pages

Internet web pages are dynamic, growing, evolving entities. Useful web pages are routinely updated, expanded, and cross-linked to similar sites. Once identified, they can be "bookmarked" for quick reference and retrieval. Many government web pages are invaluable ethnographic resources. Educational anthropologists have found the U.S. Department of Education's web pages (Figure 4.5) up-to-date and informative with regard to national policies and practices, including systemic school reform, charter schools, vouchers, school-to-work, and teacher professionalization.

Medical anthropologists can find information about the Individuals with Disabilities Act and information from the Department of Health and Human Services. Other useful government sites include the Census Bureau, the Department of Labor, NASA and NASA's K-12 Internet Initiative, Geological Survey, and the National Park Service.

Video- and Audioconferencing

Videoconferencing over the Internet is another useful way to collect data in the field. Videoconferencing software allows people or groups of individuals to see each other and talk to each other over the Internet (without

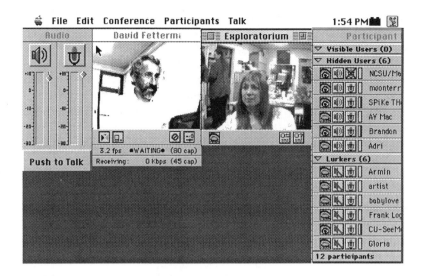

Figure 4.6. Example of Videoconferencing

SOURCE: Reproduced with permission from David Fetterman and Sally Duensing.

a long-distance telephone charge; see Figure 4.6). CU-SeeMe is free black-and-white videoconferencing software available from Cornell University. Much like a two-way radio, one person activates a "virtual button" on the screen with the cursor to speak. The other person then takes a turn and continues the conversation. This format is somewhat stilted, but after a basic introduction (and reasonable expectations concerning the quality of the interaction) it can be effective. I use this tool only after I have already established a rapport with individuals except during projects conducted completely on the Internet, such as studying on-line study groups or reflector site activities, including "chat" rooms on the Internet. It is particularly valuable half-way through or at the end of a project when additional information is needed but the travel budget is low. Videoconferencing on the Internet also provides a way to supplement periodic visits and thus maintain and strengthen field relationships. In addition, most videoconferencing software programs have a "chat" window, allowing participants to type instantaneous messages or notes to each other (this is particularly valuable when the quality of the telephone line connection is seriously degraded). Some colleagues use this software without the camera to talk and chat over the Internet. Commercial videoconferencing software programs allow speakers to talk to each other without pushing buttons (full duplex) and have "white boards" that allow users to draw diagrams on a virtual white board on their screens. I have used a white board to diagram my understanding of the organizational hierarchy in a site, and my key actor corrected me on the spot by "erasing" and "replacing" some of my lines and adding her own. I have also used this software to give talks in Michigan and other states from my office at Stanford University. (I could see my colleagues, and they projected my image on a video screen on the wall.) Clearly, this software cannot replace face-to-face communication and interactions. However, it is becoming an invaluable complement to the ethnographer's data collection tools (for additional detail, see Fetterman, 1996a, b; also see Bonk, Appleman, & Hay, 1996).

A variety of free and commercial software programs on the Internet, such as pretty good privacy (PGP) fone or Internet Phone, enable people to talk over the Internet without any picture. (Free e-mail services are offered by HotMail and RocketMail.)

Data Sharing and Analysis Tools

In addition to searching for valuable web pages and software on the Internet, ethnographers are creating web pages to share data and resources. Web pages can be created by manually using HyperText Markup Language (HTML) code or, more easily, by using one of the many freeware programs to create home pages. Claris Home Page and Page Mill are among the most user-friendly and inexpensive commercial software programs. Netscape Communicator comes with an excellent html/editor (page composer) built in. I have used these programs to create home pages about my projects, enabling my research teams to share pictures, text, and sound almost instantaneously throughout the world. For example, pictures of our sites are captured with digital cameras (cameras that automatically capture an image in a form that can be placed on the web without scanning) or by using regular cameras and then scanned or digitized and uploaded to the web. These pages (and in some cases the sites) are available only to the research team. These sites are not generally accessible; a colleague would have to know the precise location or URL. In some instances, I require a password to view them.

Listservs, such as Applied Anthropology Computer Network (ANTHAP), are e-mail distribution lists that facilitate dialogue and post announcements for large groups. When one person asks a question or makes a comment, the listserv broadcasts that message to the entire group. A member of the group has the option of broadcasting a response to the entire group or sending a personal response. It is an open, democratic way of facilitating dialogue and discussion, but can be unwieldy if it is not monitored. Ethnographically astute systems operators and facilitators know when and how to spin off specialized conversations into separate discussions limited to a subset of the listserv population interested in that topic. Members of American Anthropological Association or Society for Applied Anthropology can subscribe to the ANTHAP listserv by consulting the ANTHAP home page at http://anthap.oakland.edu/. Similarly, the Council on Anthropology and Education has a listserv titled CAE-L. ANTHRO-L is another general anthropology listserv. Members of listservs can unsubscribe at any time (when their interests shift or their time is limited) and subscribe again as desired.

VIRTUAL OFFICE
AND FILE SHARING

I also set up virtual offices and workspaces on the web to share draft memoranda and reports with colleagues. Folders on specific topics can be created on the web, much as they are on a personal computer. They can be accessed by colleagues at any time and from any place in the world with a wire or wireless modem connection. These folders help keep topics and comments organized and manageable. E-mail and listservs accomplish the same purpose but can clutter electronic mail boxes, making it difficult to retrieve comments or connect them with their reference document.

File sharing is also an option to facilitate the exchange of documents and programs. File Transfer Protocol (FTP) software can be used to transfer documents and programs from one computer to another across the Internet, such as Fetch. Telnet software enables you to log onto other computers, enabling you to use their programs and data. I have used Farallon's Timbukto Pro, commercial software, and their free but limited capability Netscape plug-in called Look@Me to facilitate data exchange and collaborate on research projects. Timbukto software enables the user to connect to other computers and be accessed by them at the same time. The Look@Me Netscape plug-in allows computer users to view each other's desktop but without the ability to manipulate files or exchange programs. In a recent study, we used the free Look@Me plug-in to allow students in the district (and potentially throughout the world) to view a science experiment—a chart of the temperature of a pond (at three depths) throughout the day. They could view the data without manipulating the program settings. Timbukto Pro was used to exchange data bases, including interviews about the experiment and temperature records. (See also pcANYWHERE32 by Symantec.)

DATABASE SOFTWARE

Traditionally, ethnographers look for patterns by sifting through the data in their heads and in their notes. This method is effective in identifying gross patterns and practices in the culture under study. It does not, however, provide strong checks and balances on conclusions. Also, sifting through old notes and records to look into the simplest hypotheses is enormously time-consuming.

Database software programs enable the ethnographer to play a multitude of what-if games and to test a variety of hypotheses with the push of a button (and a few macros—strings of commands—assigned to that button). I have used several different database programs to test my perceptions of the frequency of certain behaviors, to test specific hypotheses, and to provide new insights into the data. Qualitative software falls into several functional categories from word or text retrievers to theory testing.

BOX 4.2

Commercial Computer Programs for Ethnographic and Qualitative Data Analysis (Categories)

Programs	*Operations Performed*
Word processors, Metamorph, Orbis, Sonar Professional, The Text Collector, WordCruncher, or ZyINDEX	Word/phrase hunt or text retrieval
askSam, Folio VIEWS, Tabletop, and MAX	Organizing and sorting text systems or textbase management
HyperQual2, Kwalitan, QUALPRO, Martin, and The Ethnograph	Find and display coded data or code-and-retrieve programs
AQUAD, ATLAS/ti, HyperRESEARCH, NUD•IST, and QCA	Theory generation
ATLAS/ti, MECA, and SemNet	Theory testing

Spreadsheet and fixed-field database programs are less suitable for field notes but are useful for more limited data sets and manipulation, such as name, address, sex, ethnicity, date, and time. Many powerful and flexible systems are available for those willing to learn to use them. A significant learning curve, however, is still required to use most of them. As a rule of thumb, remember that it does not require a sledge hammer to drive a nail. The simplest and most appropriate program should be selected to complete a given task. The selection of database software should be based on the research task or purpose and ease of use. Whereas most programs enable the ethnographer to sort and compare data, NUD•IST, HyperRESEARCH, and other programs facilitate both simple sorts and comparisons and theory generation. Useful database software must be capable of manipulating long field notes and verbatim quotations. Most databases have limited and static fields. Ethnograph, NUD•IST, and HyperQual2, for example, are particularly suited to ethnographic research because they allow the ethnographer to enter long field notes without difficulty. FileMaker Pro and Dataease are not as flexible or powerful to use but are much easier to learn. NUD•IST, HyperResearch, HyperQual2, and Ethnograph allow the ethnographer to modify the coding system during analysis, change the boundaries of text segments after the initial period of data entry, and overlap coded segments.

Database programs have complemented traditional fieldwork practices in several of my studies. In one study of a health and safety department, at a Department of Energy (DOE) facility, a database was indispensable. I entered the departmental (optically scanned hard copy) accident records and conventional information, such as time, date, person, and place, into a database. I also entered the type of accident, using the department's system for recording accidents by body part. I also read descriptions of what happened in each case and entered my own classification for each accident according to the behavior associated with the event. For example, I entered a strained back resulting from lifting as a lifting accident in the database. I did not find any significant pattern of accident from records based on body parts. When I tested the database by looking for patterns based on behaviors associated with accidents, however, a number of clear patterns emerged, including accidents associated with lifting, cutting, moving, and carrying. In addition, the sorting process identified highly accident-prone individuals and indicated improperly designed workstations. This process took the computer a few moments; it would have taken me weeks to sort and re-sort by hand, an amount of time my budget did not allow. The database provided useful conventional information, such as accident type, frequency during a 10-year period, victim, behavior, and location for the most serious injuries. The database also led to new, more useful ways to conceptualize and record accidents that enable department personnel to focus their safety training dollars more effectively on the right target populations, including repeaters. Health and safety officials designed new educational programs to address identifiable behaviors most often associated with accidents and redesigned dangerous workstations. Sharing this type of information in a nonthreatening context also strengthened my relationship with facility personnel.

In another study of a teacher education program, my research team members and I entered interview data into NUD•IST and then identified and confirmed a startling pattern—the existence of an unacknowledged two-tiered faculty system with significant differences in status and financial security. In the same study, I have been experimenting with Constellations software, a free prototype database system designed to catalog, describe, and organize digital data.

Ethnographers have conducted fieldwork for generations without the benefit of laptops, desktop computers, or the Internet, and some will continue to do so. In many disciplines, however, these tools are becoming indispensable, and today few anthropologists conduct research without the use of a computer or web tool. Nevertheless, computers and the Internet have limitations: They are only as good as the data the user enters or retrieves. They still require the eyes and ears of the ethnographer to determine what to collect and how to record it as well as how to interpret the data from a cultural perspective. (See Brian Schwimmer's, 1996, review and evaluation of anthropology on the Internet in *Current Anthropology* or on the Internet.) Allen Lutins compiled a list of anthropological resources on the Internet. In addition, Fischer (1994) provides an excellent discussion about applications in computing for ethnographers. Brent (1984), Conrad and Reinharz (1984), Podolefsky and McCarthy (1983), and Sproull and Sproull (1982) also provide useful insights about computing in ethnographic and qualitative research. "Computer-Assisted Anthropology" (1984), a special section of *Practicing Anthropology,* provides another useful discussion of computers in anthropological research. A convenient table of web pages and URLs is presented at the conclusion of this chapter.

PRINTERS AND SPEAKERS

Using a computer without a printer is like playing a stereo with earphones. The user can observe the data as they are entered, edit and manipulate them in various ways, save them, and retrieve them endlessly, but sharing the data is difficult unless someone is willing to sit in front of a screen and review the material. The selection of a printer requires care and consideration of the individual's tastes, needs, and budget. An inexpensive inkjet printer is excellent for field notes, memoranda, manuscripts, and other draft-quality materials. Many new inkjet printers produce near letter-quality print. Desktop publishing quality requires a laser printer, which produces typeset-quality material quickly for immediate distribution. Typeset quality is necessary for final reports in most professional circles, including academic institutions, research corporations, government agencies, and the business community.

Speakers and microphones have become a standard part of the package. Shielded speakers protect your data from damage and screen display from distortion and provide stereo-quality sounds over the Internet–whether a key actor's voice while videoconferencing or MIDI music from the specific region under study. Microphones complete the configuration, allowing the ethnographer to make verbal notes attached to text in a word processor, conduct an interview using the laptop as a tape recorder, or communicate in an interactive videoconferencing exchange on the Internet.

This brief review of ethnographic equipment is certainly not exhaustive. For example, many novel computer-aided design tools provide three-dimensional pictures of objects—an extremely useful tool for anthropologists working in space exploration. The tools discussed in this chapter, however, are already commonly used in the field. As aids to the ethnographer's own senses and abilities, they ease the difficult task of analysis, which is the subject of Chapter 5.

BOX 4.3

The American Anthropological Association's

(http://www.ameranthassn.org/)

Anthropology Resources on the Internet Web Page

(http://www.ameranthassn.org/resinet.htm)

is one of many links to this source of information.

(continued)

BOX 4.3 (continued)

Computer Programs Used in Ethnography
Useful Freeware

CU-SeeMe http://cu-seeme.cornell.edu/	Free black-and-white videoconferencing software available from Cornell University http://www-leland.stanford.edu/~davidf/videoconference.html
MicNotePad http://moof.com/nirvana/	Freeware that turns your PowerBook into a tape recorder and facilitates transcription
PGPfone http://web.mit.edu/network/pgpfone/	Software program that enables people to talk over the Internet without any long-distance charge (and with privacy)
SchoolStat http://lucy.ukc.ac.uk/archives.html	Software to demonstrate graphically probability distributions

Prototype category:
  Constellations
 	
http://www.merlin.ubc.ca/tool/
  C25/index.html
	Prototype database system designed to catalog, describe, and organize digital data

Free E-Mail and Home Page Services

E-mail: HotMail	http://www.hotmail.com
E-mail: RocketMail	http://www.rocketmail.com
Home page: AngelFire	http://www.angelfire.com

Commercial Computer Programs
for Ethnographic Data Analysis (Contact Information)

HyperRESEARCH	617-961-3909	paul@bcvms.bc.edu
HyperQual2	602-892-9173	Raymond V. Padilla (raymond.padilla@asu.edu)

BOX 4.3 (continued)

NUD•IST	61(3)459-1699 or 805-499-0721 (SAGE/Scolari)	http://www.qsr.com.au/Nud ist-Software/nudist-descript ion.html
The Ethnograph	413-256-8835	http://www.qualisResearch. com/[qualis@mcimail.com]

Commercial Computer Programs
for Ethnographic and Qualitative
Data Analysis (Categories)

Word processors, Metamorph, Orbis, Sonar Professional, The Text Collector, WordCruncher, or ZyINDEX	Word/phrase hunt or text retrieval
askSam, Folio VIEWS, Tabletop, and MAX	Organizing and sorting text systems or textbase management
HyperQual2, Kwalitan, QUALPRO, Martin, and The Ethnograph	Find and display coded data or code-and-retrieve programs
AQUAD, ATLAS/ti, HyperRESEARCH, NUD•IST, and QCA	Theory generation
ATLAS/ti, MECA, and SemNet	Theory testing

See Weitzman and Miles (1995) for
more discussion about these categories
and a review of each of these software
programs for qualitative data analysis.

Internet Searcher Pages

AltaVista	http://altavista.digital.com/
Excite	http://www.excite.com/
HotBot	http://www.hotbot.com/
Yahoo	http://www.yahoo.com/

Internet Reference Pages

Libray of Congress	http://www.loc.gov/
The Federal Web Locator	http://www.law.vill.edu/Fed-Agency/fedw ebloc.html
The New York Times Navigator	http://www.nytimes.com/library/cyber/ref erence/cynavi.html
Smithsonian Institution	http://www.si.edu/newstart.htm
Xplore	http://www.xplore.com/xplore500/medium /reference.html

(continued)

BOX 4.3 (continued)
Directory Assistance Pages

Four11	http://www.four11.com/
LookupUSA	http://www.lookupusa.com/
MapsOnUs	http://www.MapsOnUs.com
MapQuest	http://www.mapquest.com
Switchboard	http://www.switchboard.com
Zip2	http://www.Zip2.com/

Freeware and Shareware Collections

Father of Shareware	http://www.halcyon.com/knopf/jim
TUCOWS Collection of Internet Software	http://www.tucows.com

Practical References (While in the Field)

Currency Converters	http://www.olsen.ch/cgi-bin/exmenu
MedicineNet (free medical resources)	http://www.medicinenet.com/

File Transfer Software

Fetch (Macintosh and Windows)	http://www.dartmouth.edu/pages/softdev/ fetch.html or http://www.fetchsoft.com
WSFTP (Windows)	http://tucows.phx.cox.com/files/ ws_ftp32.zip
Look@Me	http://www.farallon.com
pcANYWHERE32	http://www.sos.symantec.com/faq/Pcawin 32.html
Timbukto Pro	http://www.farallon.com

Voice Recognition Software

Dragon PowerSecretary Personal Edition	http://www.speechrec.com/WhatIsPS.html
IMB Voice Type Dictation Software (Gold)	http://www.voicerecognition.com/ibm/ibm des.html

Videocam Connections Worldwide

Bill's Random Camera	http://www.xmission.com:80/~bill/cgi-bin / camera-list.cgi
EarthCam	http://www.earthcam.com
Live Cam Pictures World Wide (provides a list of locations from Antarctica to the United Kingdom)	http://www.wsu.edu:8000/~i9248809/ anthrop.html (and then select pictures worldwide)

BOX 4.3 (continued)

Peeping Tom (Europe, North America, and world locations) — http://www.csd.uu.se/~s96fst/

Selected Government Web Pages

Census Bureau	http://www.census.gov/
Department of Education	http://www.ed.gov/
Individuals with Disabilities Act	http://www.ed.gov/IDEA/
Department of Health and Human Services	http://www.os.dhhs.gov/
Department of Labor	http://www.dol.gov/
Geological Survey	http://www.usgs.gov/
NASA	http://www.nasa.gov/
NASA's K-12 Internet Initiative	http://quest.arc.nasa.gov/
National Park Service	http://www.nps.gov/

Selected Ethnographic Sites
Professional Organizations

American Anthropological Association	http://www.ameranthassn.org/
Society for Applied Anthropology	http://www.telepath.com/sfaa/
Society for Medical Anthropology	http://www.people.memphis.edu/~sma/
Society for Visual Anthropology	http://custwww.xensei.com/docued/sva/

Academic Organizations

Anthropology resources	http://www.usd.edu:80/anth
Anthropology resources at the University of Kent	http://lucy.ukc.ac.uk:80/index.html
Department of Anthropology of the University of Geneva, Switzerland	http://anthropologie.unige.ch:80
Ethnographics Laboratory USC (visual anthropology focus)	http://www.usc.edu/dept/elab/welcome/
San Francisco State University Anthropology Department	http://www.sfsu.edu:80/~anthro
UCSB anthropology web site	http://www.sscf.ucsb.edu:80/anth/
UpDate	http://www2.uu.se:80/insts/antro/bh

Collections

Anthropology (Texas A&M)	gopher://gopher.tamu.edu:70/11/.dir/anthropology.dir
Naked Scientific Archaeology and Co-Ed Physical Anthropology page	http://www.caverns.com/~catiline/index.html

(continued)

BOX 4.3 (continued)

Nicole's AnthroPage	http://www.wsu.edu:8000/~i9248809/
University of Michigan Museum of Anthropology	http://www.umma.lsa.umich.edu:80
William Calvin's books and articles	http://weber.u.washington.edu:80/~wcalvin

Directories

Anthropology and Archaeology Corner	gopher://rsl.ox.ac.uk/11/anthro-corn
Deaf Resource Library (Yale)	http://pantheon.yale.edu/~nakamura/deaf/
HELLENIC CIVILIZATION—Ariadne Network Gopher	gopher://ithaki.servicenet.ariadne-t.gr/11/ HELLENIC_CIVILIZATION
Library of Congress (LC MARVEL) (Anthropology Collection)	gopher://marvel.loc.gov/11/global/socsci/
Peabody Museum (Yale)	gopher://gopher.peabody.yale.edu:70/
Polynesian Voyaging Society—University of Hawaii	gopher://nic2.hawaii.net/11/PVS
RiceInfo (Rice University CWIS) (Anthropology Collection)	gopher://riceinfo.rice.edu/11/
Texas A&M Anthropology Collection	gopher://gopher.tamu.edu/11/.dir/anthropology.dir
The World-Wide Web Virtual Library: Anthropology	http://www.usc.edu:80/dept/v-lib/anthropology.html
University of California at Berkeley, Library Anthropology Collection	gopher://infolib.lib.berkeley.edu/11/resdbs/
University of Kent at Canterbury, Social Anthropology Archive	gopher://lucy.ukc.ac.uk
University of Texas at Dallas (Anthropology Collection)	gopher://gopher.utdallas.edu/11/
World Wide Anthropology Resources	http://sosig.esrc.bris.ac.uk/Subjects/anthro.html
Yahoo's Directory—Anthropology and Archeology	http://www.yahoo.com/Social_Science/ Anthropology_and_Archaeology/
Fetterman's Ethnography and the Internet page	http://www-leland.stanford.edu/~davidf/ ethnography.html

Film Resource

Documentary educational resource	http://der.org/docued/

On-Line Journals

Cultural Dynamics	http://dynamics.rug.ac.be/home.htm
Education Policy Analysis Archives (education policy)	http://olam.ed.asu.edu/epaa/

BOX 4.3 (continued)

Journal of Political Ecology	gopher://dizzy.library.arizona.edu:70/11/ ej/PE/jpe
Journal of World Anthropology	gopher://wings.buffalo.edu:70/h0/academic /department/anthropology/jwa/index
Journal of World Systems	http://csf.colorado.edu/wsystems/jwsr.html
Qualitative Report	http://www.nova.edu/ssss/QR/index.html
Committee on Institutional Cooperation Electronic Journals Collection	http://ejournals.cic.net

Selected Anthropological Listservs

ANTHAP home page	Society for Applied Anthropology/AAA listserv http://anthap.oakland.edu/
ANTHRO-L	General anthropology listserv
CAE-L	Council on Anthropology and Education listserv

Reviews and References Concerning
Qualitative Research, Software, and the Internet

Fetterman's ethnography and the Internet web page provides a routinely updated version of this chapter in the new edition of *Ethnography: Step by Step* (second edition)	http://www-leland.stanford.edu/~davidf/ ethnography.html
Fischer (1994) provides an excellent discussion about applications in computing for ethnographers	Fetterman (1996c)
Lutins compiled a list of anthropological resources on the Internet	http://www.nitehawk.com/alleycat/ anth-faq.html
Schwimmer (1996) reviews and evaluates anthropology on the Internet	Also available at http://www.artsci.wustl.edu/~anthro/ca/ papers/schwimmer/intro.html
Weitzman and Miles (1995) provide an excellent presentation of computer programs for qualitative data analysis	

NOTE

1. Although users are experiencing problems with the bandwidth at the time of this writing, the Next Generation Internet and Internet 2 will use high-speed fiberoptic circuits, coaxial cables, or satellite transmission, and higher quality software significantly enhancing access to the Web. Videoconferencing will benefit greatly from these improvements and will become a "normal" mode of computer communication in the near future.

5

Finding Your Way Through the Forest: Analysis

*I went to the woods because I wished to live deliberately,
to front only the essential facts of life, and see if
I could not learn what it had to teach.*
—Henry David Thoreau

Analysis is one of the most engaging features of ethnography. It begins from the moment a fieldworker selects a problem to study and ends with the last word in the report or ethnography. Ethnography involves many levels of analysis. Some are simple and informal; others require some statistical sophistication. Ethnographic analysis is iterative, building on ideas throughout the study. Analyzing data in the field enables the ethnographer to know precisely which methods to use and when and how to use them. Analysis tests hypotheses and perceptions to construct an accurate conceptual framework about what is happening in the social group. Analysis in ethnography is as much a test of the ethnographer as it is a test of the data.

The fieldworker must find a way through a forest of data, theory, observation, and distortion. Throughout the analytic trek, the fieldworker must make choices—between logical and enticing paths, between valid and invalid but fascinating data, and between genuine patterns of behavior and series of apparently similar but distinct reactions. Choosing the right path requires discrimination, experience, attention to both detail and the larger context, and intuition. The best guide through the thickets of analysis is at once the most obvious and most complex of strategies: clear thinking.

THINKING

First and foremost, analysis is a test of the ethnographer's ability to think—to process information meaningfully and usefully. The ethnographer confronts a vast array of complex information and needs to make some sense of it all piece by piece. The initial stage in analysis involves simple perception. Even perception, however, is selective. The ethnographer selects and isolates pieces of information from all the data in the field. The ethnographer's personal or idiosyncratic approach, together with an assortment of academic theories and models, focuses and limits the scope of inquiry. The field presents a vast amount of material, however, and in understanding day-to-day human interaction elementary thinking skills are as important as ethnographic concepts and methods.

A focus on relevant, manageable topics is essential and is possible through the refinement of the unit of analysis. The fieldworker, however, must probe those topics by comparing and contrasting data, trying to fit pieces of data into the bigger puzzle, while at the same time hypothesizing about the best fit and the best picture.

Many useful techniques, from triangulation to use of statistical software packages requiring powerful computers, help the ethnographer to make sense of the forests of data. All these techniques, however, require critical thinking skills—notably, the ability to synthesize and evaluate information—and a large dose of common sense.

TRIANGULATION

Triangulation is basic in ethnographic research. It is at the heart of ethnographic validity—testing one source of information against another to strip away alternative explanations and prove a hypothesis. Typically, the ethnographer compares information sources to test the quality of the information (and the person sharing it), to understand more completely the part an actor plays in the social drama, and ultimately to put the whole situation into perspective.

During my study of dropouts, students often showed me their grades. One young friend told me he earned straight A's that semester. I compared his verbal information with a written transcript, the teacher's verbal confirmation, and unsolicited information from his peers. His grades were excellent, but information from his teacher and his peers suggested an "attitude problem." According to them, "success went to his head." Thus, one program goal (better grades) had a problematic side effect (an overbearing attitude). This outcome was in conflict with another program goal: cooperation and harmonious relationships with others in the program. This piece of information was extremely useful to me in understanding the strengths and weaknesses of the program. In this case, triangulation not only verified the student's claims about his grades but also provided useful data about his role in the program. This information became more important in later conversations, in which he provided data that were more difficult to verify using conventional inquiry methods. A natural by-product of triangulation in this example was additional documentation about the student's overall growth or progress in the program as well as about the health of the program overall.

Triangulation works with any topic, in any setting, and on any level. It is as effective in studying the high school classroom as it is in studying higher-education administration. The trick is to compare comparable items and levels during analysis. In studying postsecondary institutions, I usually break down my unit of analysis into manageable pieces, such as school, department, or laboratory. Then I select the most significant concerns that emerged during the initial review period. I focus on those concerns throughout the study, refining my understanding of them by working with people in the field. I confirm some hypotheses, learn about new dimensions of the problems, and crystallize my overall conception of how the place operates by constantly triangulating information. Later, I use triangulated information about an individual faculty member and generalize some of these data to universitywide concerns.

One faculty member complained about the lack of funding for his laboratory during a funding hiatus while he was between grants. A review of past records and interviews with other principal investigators (to learn what they thought of the situation) and with other faculty members (to discover what they had done during past crises) revealed that his concern was widespread. Funding crises had a direct impact on the principal investigator's ability to maintain continuity in the department. A principal investigator's research program can come to a grinding halt without funds to pay the researchers. A comparison of this faculty member's complaint with other faculty complaints and internal memoranda established that funding was a real problem for the research laboratories and merited further investigation. Additional interviews with various government agency officials and university deans revealed that, from a bureaucratic perspective, the problem was merely a paperwork issue. Whether to fund a certain project was not in question. The bureaucratic structure simply created normal delays in processing renewal papers for additional funding. Therefore, the issue was really how to handle a paperwork delay and not how to survive between grants. The difference between these two situations is enormous. In most cases, money for these laboratories was promised and would be coming to the principal investigator eventually. One dean indicated that he was already aware of and working on this problem. Unfortunately, he had never discussed it with other deans, directors, or principal investigators. Thus, the principal investigators and their researchers were left to worry about what was essentially a paper problem. The larger issue that emerged from this triangulation effort was the lack of communication within the school and between the school and a variety of government agencies. The right hand did not know what the left hand was doing. Here, the by-products of triangulation were as useful as its primary use in validating information.

Triangulation always improves the quality of data and the accuracy of ethnographic findings. During my emergency room study, triangulation was invaluable in clearing up an elementary misunderstanding. The department's assistant director complained about one of the residents during an interview: "If you want to find fraud, you should look at Henry. Henry works half the time he is supposed to for twice the pay." This information came from a presumably credible source. I thought it odd, however, that given his role in the organization, he had not acted on this information. Fortunately, a bookkeeper overheard the assistant director's comment and pulled me aside the next day to say, "I thought you should know Henry is one of our best doctors. The only reason the [assistant director] bad-mouths him is because Henry is dating his ex-wife." Observations of the assistant director's ex-wife picking up Henry at the end of his shift, a review of the time records, and interviews with the nurses and the director all confirmed the bookkeeper's information. In this case, both serendipitous and systematic triangulation were invaluable in providing a reality test and a baseline of understanding.

Triangulation can occur naturally in conversation as easily as it can occur in intensive investigatory work. The ethnographer, however, must identify it in subtle contexts. A recent discussion during a meeting with school superintendents in Washington, D.C., illustrates this point. A prominent superintendent, managing one of the largest districts in the nation, had just finished explaining why school size made no difference in education. He said that he had one 1,500-pupil school and one 5,000-pupil school in his district of which he was particularly proud, and that the school size had no effect on school spirit, the educative process, or his ability to manage. He also explained that he had to build two or three new schools in the next year—either three small schools or one small school and one large one. A colleague interrupted to ask which he preferred. The superintendent replied, "Small ones, of course; they are much easier to handle." He had betrayed himself in this one phrase. Although the administrative party line was that size made no difference—management is management no matter how big or small the unit—this superintendent revealed a very different personal opinion in response to a casual question. Such self-contained triangulation, in which an individual's own statements support or undermine his or her stated position, is a useful measure of internal consistency. Later comments by this administrator continued to undermine his official position. He said that students in the small school blamed their athletic losses on school size. One student stated, "The big schools have the resources." This brief anecdote provided an additional insight into the district cosmology. Although people held different views about ideal school size, the issue of size was a critical focal point shared by all—from student to superintendent. This type of information provides a handle that aids the ethnographer in grasping a community's fundamental ideas and values. (See Webb, Campbell, Schwartz, & Sechrest, 1966, for a detailed discussion about triangulation.)

PATTERNS

Ethnographers look for patterns of thought and behavior. Patterns are a form of ethnographic reliability. Ethnographers see patterns of thought and action repeat in various situations and with various players. Looking for patterns is a form of analysis. The ethnographer begins with a mass of undifferentiated ideas and behavior and then collects pieces of information, comparing, contrasting, and sorting gross categories and minutiae until a discernible thought or behavior becomes identifiable. Next, the ethnographer must listen and observe and then compare his or her observations with this poorly defined model. Exceptions to the rule emerge and variations on a theme are detectable. These variants help to circumscribe the activity and clarify its meaning. The process requires further sifting and sorting to make a match between categories. The theme or ritualistic activity finally emerges and consists of a collection of such matches between the model (abstracted from reality) and the ongoing observed reality.

Any cultural group's patterns of thought and behavior are interwoven strands. As soon as the ethnographer finishes analyzing and identifying one pattern, another pattern emerges for analysis and identification. The fieldworker can then compare the two patterns. In practice, the ethnographer works simultaneously on many patterns. The level of understanding increases geometrically as the ethnographer moves up the conceptual ladder—mixing and matching patterns and building theory from the ground up. (See Glaser & Strauss, 1967, for a discussion of grounded theory.)

Observation of the daily activity of a middle-class family might reveal several patterns. The couple drops off their child at the day care facility and goes to work every day. They receive their paychecks every other week. Rituals such as grocery shopping and doing laundry occur every weekend. Combining these preliminary patterns into a meaningful whole makes other patterns apparent. The stresses and strains of a family in which both husband and wife must hold down full-time jobs and bring up a family, the emphasis on organization and planning, even of usually spontaneous activities, and a variety of other behaviors and practices become more meaningful and understandable in this context. The observer can make preliminary inferences about the entire economic system by analyzing the behavior that is subsumed within the patterns and the patterns themselves. Ethnographers acquire a deeper understanding of and appreciation for a culture as they weave each part of the ornate human tapestry together by observing and analyzing the patterns of everyday life.

The process of identifying and matching patterns and building theory is facilitated by the database programs discussed in Chapter 4, such as NUD•IST, The Ethnograph, and HyperQual2. For example, I have used NUD•IST software to organize raw field notes and search for patterns. The field notes were first converted into text or ASCII files and then placed in a raw data folder. With NUD•IST, I could search for key words or strings of words in all the field notes. All the examples (within the context of the paragraph within which each is found) were consolidated into one document for review and discussion to determine whether each was an appropriate example or if the contexts of the various examples were similar. Another approach is to label specific paragraphs in field notes based on their meaning. This is typically referred to as coding chunks of data. It is more time-consuming than a word search, but it is more precise and powerful. Searching for and sorting these labeled paragraphs generates a more precise list of similar examples. For example, in one study of a teacher education program, the ethnographic team searched for the code "gang" and found many references to gangs in the field notes that established a clear pattern in our data. NUD•IST generated a "report" listing all the examples. It also enabled us to create subcategories. The software facilitated the creation of gang subcatagories as well. NUD•IST also organized the data in a hierarchical tree format, allowing us to visualize how the pieces fit together as we built a picture of the program we were studying.

Database software programs such as NUD•IST set the stage for pattern identification simply by organizing the data so that you know what you have, where it is, and how you are categorizing it—all at a glance. In addition, it helps make explicit what ethnographers do in their heads all the time: sorting, comparing, searching for patterns, and building models. In some ways, the software helps demystify pattern identification and analysis by clearly articulating the coding, searching, and sorting process. It is similar to creating an index for a book. Certain patterns emerge and are documented by the frequency of page citations for each idea or author. Data entry and coding are no less time-consuming than index cards or the creation of an index. Manual sorting, however, is time-consuming and labor-intensive. With a database program, data, once entered, can be sorted frequently and effortlessly. Database software also provide a systematic form of triangulation, helping keep the ethnographer honest by providing direct access to the raw data in context and noting the frequency of the item almost instantly.

A computer screen snapshot of the results of a NUD•IST data sort from the study of the teacher education program is shown in Figure 5.1. This software helps the researcher manage a large database with visual clarity and to track the categories that emerge during this phase and throughout the project.

KEY EVENTS

Key or focal events that the fieldworker can use to analyze an entire culture occur in every social group. Geertz (1973) eloquently used the cockfight to understand and portray Balinese life. Key events come in all shapes and sizes. Some tell more about a culture than others, but all provide a focus for analysis (see also Geertz, 1957).

Key events, like snapshots or videotapes, concretely convey a wealth of information. Some images are clear representations of social activity, whereas others provide a tremendous amount of embedded meaning. Once the event is recorded, the ethnographer can enlarge or reduce any portion of the picture. A rudimentary knowledge of the social situation will enable

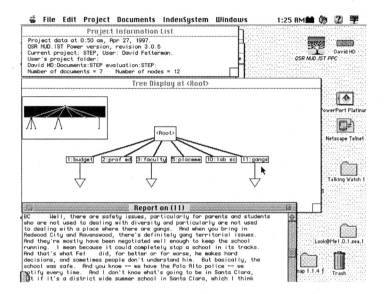

Figure 5.1. The "project information list" provides information about the number of documents and nodes (or categories). The "tree display" window provides an image of how the data are classified and categorized. For example, one category of data focuses on the budget, another on professional education schools, the third on the faculty, and so on. The arrow on the right indicates the existence of additional categories. (The entire structure of the database can be viewed in the small tree in the left-hand corner of that window.) Arrows going down from the "1: budget" and "3: faculty" categories indicate subcategories. Finally, the information at the bottom of the screen image is the actual interview data that have been coded under the faculty domain or category.

SOURCE: Reproduced with permission from QSR NUD•IST. Copyright 1985-1997, Qualitative Solutions & Research Pty. Ltd., Victoria, Australia.

the ethnographer to infer a great deal from key events. In many cases, the event is a metaphor for a way of life or a specific social value. Key events provide a lens through which to view a culture. They range from the ritual observance of the sabbath to the emergency response to a burning building in a small kibbutz. The sabbath is a ritualized key event that occurs every week. Ceremonial garb (or lack thereof), the orchestration of prayers, and the social activity that follows the service provide a highly condensed version of the culture's religious life. A fire is a key event that compels the ethnographer to observe, analyze, and act simultaneously. A participant observer has conflicting obligations. The ideal stance is simply to observe and record what happens in such a situation, but as a participant the researcher has an ethical obligation to help put out the fire. These obligations need not be mutually exclusive, however. Typically, the ethnographer simply joins in at the appropriate level depending on the danger, the amount of experience in the field with a certain group, and the behavioral norms in that situation. A fire in a small kibbutz settlement brings everyone running out of their houses to form a bucket brigade until the heavy fire-fighting equipment arrives. Involvement in this situation allows simultaneous observation and analysis. Informal leadership roles become apparent in such a crisis. The event is also a test of the cooperation on which the community professes to depend. The technological sophistication of the people who fight the fire is a good indicator of their knowledge, values, economic resources, and degree of social interaction or isolation from the mainstream. Other rare events, such as funerals, weddings, and rites of passage, also offer excellent opportunities for in-depth analysis.

A classic key event in modern offices is the introduction of computers. Individuals act out most of the hidden dimensions of social life in these situations. Formal and informal hierarchies become apparent through action and memoranda. Who decides who will have a computer? Who will use a computer as a status symbol first and a functional piece of equipment last? Subterranean tensions that have nothing to do with computers and that remain buried in daily interaction come to the surface during such key events. Observing the schism between people who fear this innovation and those who embrace it, how staff members accept or reject the computer, and how its use changes the group's social dynamics can be an all-consuming but revealing task.

For example, a fistfight erupted during a basketball game at one of the Career Intern Program (CIP) sites. On the surface, this key event indicated the volatility of the social group and the occasion. On a deeper level, the fight was more revealing about the program's social dynamics. One fighter had been in the program for some time; the other was new. The new member threatened to have his group take over the program and "trash it." The old member was protective of the program, viewing it, as his peers did, as "a big family." Thus, he protected the program in a way both parties would understand. The fight was actually a minidrama in the bigger struggle between the two groups. It was also a rite of passage into the program: The display of loyalty said more about the program to the new participants than the fight itself.

Key events are extraordinarily useful for analysis. Not only do they help the fieldworker understand a social group but also the fieldworker in turn can use them to explain the culture to others. The key event thus becomes a metaphor for the culture. Key events also illustrate how participation, observation, and analysis are inextricably bound together during fieldwork.

MAPS

Visual representations are useful tools in ethnographic research. Having to draw a map of the community tests an ethnographer's understanding of the area's physical layout. It can also help the ethnographer chart a course through the community. Like writing, mapmaking forces the ethnographer to abstract and reduce reality to a manageable size—a piece of paper. The process of drawing also crystallizes images, networks, and understandings and suggests new paths to explore. Maps, flowcharts, and matrices all help to crystallize and display consolidated information.

FLOWCHARTS

Flowcharts are useful in studies of production line operations. Mapping out what happens to a book in a research library, from the time it is received on the shipping dock to the time it is cataloged and available on the shelf, can provide a baseline of understanding about the system. Flowcharting a social welfare program is also common in evaluation. The analytic process of mapping the flow of activity and information can also serve as a vehicle to initiate additional discussions.

ORGANIZATIONAL CHARTS

Drawing organizational charts—of a program, department, library, or kibbutz—is a useful analytic tool, as discussed in Chapter 2 under "Structure and Function." It tests the ethnographer's knowledge of the system in the same manner as does drawing a map or a flowchart. Both formal and informal organizational hierarchies can be charted for comparison. In addition, organizational charts can measure changes as people move in and out or up and down the hierarchy. Organizational charts clarify the structure and function of any institutional form of human organization.

MATRICES

Matrices provide a simple, systematic, graphic way to compare and contrast data. The researcher can compare and cross-reference categories of information to establish a picture of a range of behaviors or thought categories. Matrices also help the researcher to identify emerging patterns in the data.

The construction of a matrix was valuable during the first stage of my study of state-funded art programs. Art programs fell into various categories, such as music, dance, theater, painting, and sculpture; these categories became column titles on a spreadsheet. The rows consisted of other categories: geographic location, size, funds, consortia, and other relevant variables. I located the specific programs in the appropriate boxes or cells. This exercise provided an immediate picture of the range of variation across programs, the types of program in each category, geographic clusters, and many other valuable pieces of information. In addition, these data helped me to select a smaller, stratified sample within the population for in-depth fieldwork.

Similarly, a matrix helped to identify themes across sites during the dropout study. Rites of passage were noted in the appropriate cell. By designing the matrix according to academic calendar years, I could record changes. The researcher can develop a matrix by hand on paper, on a spreadsheet (paper or software), or with the assistance of a database software program. (See Miles & Huberman, 1984, for a detailed presentation of the use of matrices in qualitative research.)

CONTENT ANALYSIS

Ethnographers analyze written and electronic data in much the same way that they analyze observed behavior. They triangulate information within documents to test for internal consistency. They attempt to discover patterns within the text and seek key events recorded and memorialized in words.

The dropout program study produced volumes of written records to review: teaching and counseling manuals, administrative guides, research reports, newspaper articles, magazine articles, and hundreds of memoranda. Internal documents received special scrutiny to determine whether they were internally consistent with program philosophy. The review revealed significant patterns. For example, the role of religion in these programs was evident. The literature contained testimonial statements that the program owed its success to the "direct involvement of religious leaders." Lease agreements often specified a church in which to house the program. Letters from the organization's leader, himself a minister, were written in pastoral tones.

Similarly, the program philosophy was easy to detect after a study of the program's public documents in conjunction with daily observation. The program espoused a self-help, middle-class approach to life with a flavor of the Puritan ethic. Program pamphlets contained routine references to "the work ethic," "individual responsibility for success," "marketable skills," and enabling the disenfranchised to "claim their fair share of the [economic] pie." In numerous instances, I recorded certain words and phrases to determine their frequency in the text. I often inferred the significance of a concept from its frequency and context. The program's magazine articles, editorials, and memoranda documented key events such as civil rights legislation, reverse discrimination court cases, racial incidents, and local ethnic events. The organization's official position on these events told much about its politics and fundamental values.

The ethnographer can analyze data culled from electronic media in precisely the same fashion as he or she can analyze written documentation. Because this material is often in a database or in a format that can easily transfer into a database, extensive manipulation—sorting, comparing, contrasting, aggregating, and synthesizing—is even simpler. In my higher-education studies, most content analysis takes place on-line or after downloading to a database. Management philosophy is easily detected in on-line meeting minutes, budgets, arguments, and policy statements (and drafts). A brief review of a department's budget provides vital information about its values: People put their money into areas they care about. A comparison of content analysis data with interview and observational data can significantly enhance the quality of findings.

STATISTICS

Ethnographers often collect data that are in the form of frequencies ("how many times did the director address the staff as 'guys'?" and "How often does the gang change hand signals in a 6-month period?"), ranks ("What is the order of the six administrators in power within the organization?"), or quantified names ("Agnostics are scored '1', Fundamentalists are scored '2', etc."). Like sociologists, political scientists, and many other social scientists, ethnographers seldom resort to well-established metrics, such as the gram-centimeter-second world of the physical sciences or even the IQ scale and test scores of the psychologist. As a consequence of this measurement style, ethographers usually employ methods of statistical analysis that more resemble the sociologist's chi-square contingency table analysis or rank correlations and distribution-free tests (Friedman Rank Test, Mann-Whitney U test, etc.) than they resemble the analysis of variances, t tests, and regression analyses of the psychologist or economist.

Anthropologists typically work with nominal and ordinal scales. Nominal scales consist of discrete categories, such as sex and religion. Ordinal scales also provide discrete categories as well as a range of variation within each category—for example, reform, conservative, and orthodox variants within the category of Judaism. Ordinal scales do not determine the degree of difference among subcategories.

The Guttman (1944) scale is one example of a useful ordinal scale in ethnographic research. In studying folk medicators, I used a Guttman scale to illustrate pictorially the range of attitudes toward the use of modern Western medicine from most receptive to most resistant to change in the community. A correlation of the Guttman scale scores with such variables as age, education, immigration status, and related value system variables identified population segments that would be most interested in educational material about alternative medicating practices. This information provided a target group and suggested an efficient use of limited educational resources while respecting the wishes of those who were not interested in learning more about modern medicating practices. (See Pelto, 1970, for additional discussion of the Guttman scale.)

Likert scales provide an advance in reliability, validity, and ease of use over the Guttman scale. A typical Likert survey scale is based on a 5-point rating system. For example, concerning the topic "support and guidance in securing employment," excellent was 5, satisfactory was 3, and poor was 1 on the scale. The Likert survey scale was easy to administer, and analysis consisted of calculating the mode, mean, and range. The survey questions were based on individual interviews and focus groups, grounding the questions in the students' perception of the program. The survey provided some degree of generalizability or representativeness concerning student opinions about the program. The survey findings, in combination with interviews and observations, made for credible and persuasive conclusions about the "consumer's view" of the program.

A chi-square test provided an insight into enrollment trends in the study of gifted and talented education programs. The test indicated that Hispanics had the most statistically significant increase in that program (Fetterman, 1988a). Another popular nonparametric statistical tool in anthropology is the Fisher's Exact Probability Test. All statistical formulas, however, require that certain assumptions are met before application to any situation. A disregard for these variables in the statistical equation is as dangerous as neglect of comparable assumptions in the human equation in conducting ethnographic fieldwork. Both errors result in distorted and misleading efforts at worst and waste valuable time at best.

Ethnographers also use the results of parametric statistics, as well as test scores, to test certain hypotheses, cross-check their own observations, and generally provide additional insight. Student test scores were essential to one portion of the CIP study. The sponsors wanted to know if the students' reading and math capabilities improved as a result of their participation in the program. Gains in reading scores were statistically significant. From the sponsors' and the ethnographer's perspective, this information was a useful finding. The gains in math scores were statistically significant but less spectacular than the gains in reading scores. This particular finding provided the ethnographer a unique opportunity to interact with the psychometrician in a significant—interpretive—fashion. The statistical calculation delivered an outcome but not the process behind it. Ethnographic description was useful in explaining why the math gains were not as spectacular as those in reading. The answer was simple: The math teaching positions were vacant during most of the study. The program had difficulty recruiting and maintaining math teachers given the competitive market for these individuals.

The test outcomes were a product of traditional psychometric approaches, including control and comparison group data using analysis of covariance and standardized gain procedures. This information was both useful to sponsors and the ethnographer and valuable in providing a focal point for further inquiry and data comparison.

In addition to commercial statistics packages, such as SPSS, I use a shareware program called SchoolStat (Figure 5.2). One of its strengths is its ability to graphically demonstrate probability distributions. It also has a spreadsheet, facilitating sorting, arithmetic and mathematical transformations (including z or N scores), statistical tests including descriptive statistics, confidence intervals, paired and independent comparisons (parametric and nonparametric), correlations, linear regression, and contingency tables. SchoolStat generates scatterplots, histograms, boxplots, stem and leaf diagrams, and pie charts. It includes both static probability tables (e.g., normal, t and F distribution, and chi-square distribution) and active tables. This software can be found at the University of Kent's Centre for Social

Anthropology and Computing software server at http://lucy.ukc.ac.uk/archives.html.

Problems With Statistics

The use of statistics in ethnography has many problems. Meeting the assumptions that a specific test requires may be a particularly sticky problem. One of the most common assumptions of inferential statistics is that the sample is random. Typically, ethnography uses stratified judgmental sampling rather than a truly randomized selection. The use of parametric statistics requires large samples. Most ethnographers work with small groups, however. The issues of expertise and appropriateness raise further difficulties.

In many instances, sophisticated statistical approaches are inappropriate in ethnography in particular and in social science in general. The first criterion is the appropriateness of the tool for the problem. The second criterion—a subset of the first—is the methodological soundness of the application. A third criterion involves ethics. Is use of a certain tool at a given time with a certain population ethical? The ethical question is discussed in Chapter 7.

No design or technique is good or bad per se. The application, however, can be useful or useless and appropriate or inappropriate. The use of an experimental design and related statistical formulas to study the impact of an educational program or treatment on a population of former dropouts, near dropouts, and "push outs" (those the schools are no longer obligated to serve because they are too old or too disruptive) is conceptually sound. In the abstract, this approach could shed light on possible gains in math and reading scores by students in the program (compared with scores of students in the control group). The application of this design to generate sophisticated statistical inferences about most educational programs, however, is inappropriate on strict methodological grounds. The assumptions of the design are rarely met. A most valid experimental design with human subjects involves a double-blind arrangement. The individual delivering the treatment, the individual receiving it, and the individual in the control group do not know who is really receiving treatment. In most educational treatments, teachers know whether or not they are delivering an educational treatment, and the students know whether or not they have been accepted into the educational program. Instead of a double-blind experiment, the treatment group receives a positive treatment; rejected students receive a negative treatment. Thus, students receiving treatment may react with a Hawthorne effect, whereas rejected students may react with a John Henry

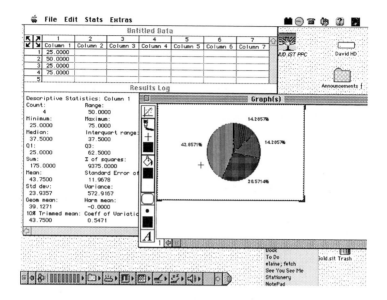

Figure 5.2. Example of the SchoolStat Program
SOURCE: Reproduced with permission from David Darby.

effect—overcompensating to demonstrate that they can do well despite the rejection. These forms of reactivity and contamination severely undermine the credibility of any outcome (see Fetterman, 1982b, for a detailed discussion of this problem; see also Cook & Campbell, 1979).

Another problem with statistical tests is perceptual. Statistics demonstrate correlations and not causality. People frequently fall into the trap of inferring causality from statistical correlation, however. Also, as Mark Twain wrote, "There are three kinds of lies—lies, damned lies, and statistics." A competent individual can manipulate figures to indicate almost anything. Statistical findings can be mesmerizing for some individuals. Computer-generated findings are 10 times as credible for no better reason than technological sophistication. Computer-generated statistical errors can be particularly troublesome (if not materially significant) because they are reproduced incorrectly throughout related databases for long periods of time before detection. Countervailing forces or tests cannot easily compensate for such systemic problems.

This brief review of problems should not dampen the spirits of an enterprising ethnographer. Ethnography has ample use for experimental designs, quasi-experimental designs, and associated statistical analyses, including multiple regression analysis and factor analysis (Britan, 1978; Maxwell, Bashook, & Sandlow, 1986). This brief review merely highlights the complexity that statistical analyses can create in ethnography or any other social science (for a useful presentation of statistics for the social sciences, see Blalock, 1979; Hopkins, Hopkins, & Glass, 1996; Shavelson, 1996).

CRYSTALLIZATION

Ethnographers crystallize their thoughts at various stages throughout an ethnographic endeavor. The crystallization may bring a mundane conclusion, a novel insight, or an earth-shaking epiphany. The crystallization is typically the result of a convergence of similarities that spontaneously strike the ethnographer as relevant or important to the study. Crystallization may be an exciting process or the result of painstaking, boring, methodical work. This research gestalt requires attention to all pertinent variables in an equation. Gross errors can be misleading and lethal to any investigation. For example, a long line of cars with their lights on, all proceeding down the same street in the same direction, might suggest a funeral procession. However logical this conclusion might appear, it may also be dead wrong. Additional data from informal interviews or more disciplined and detailed observations are necessary. For example, identification of a hearse in the procession or a confirming word from one of the individuals involved would immeasurably improve the credibility of this conclusion. Another significant piece of information involves time. If the observer leaves out one vital piece of information—for example, that the researcher saw this long chain of cars with their lights on at night—the credibility and probability of this conclusion are severely eroded. Participation at the funeral itself lends a great deal of face validity to the conclusion or crystallized conception.

Every study has classic moments when everything falls into place. After months of thought and immersion in the culture, a special configuration forms. All the subtopics, mini-experiments, layers of triangulated effort, key events, and patterns of behavior form a coherent and often cogent picture of what is happening. One of the most exciting moments in ethnographic research is when an ethnographer discovers a counterintuitive conception of reality—a conception that defies common sense. Such moments make the long days and nights worthwhile. During a recent study of research administration in higher education, I found after months of work that the situation had a counterintuitive solution. The administration consisted of two separate divisions serving separate departments in the university. The director of the two divisions was contemplating merging them into one unit. Logically, the merger would achieve greater efficiency by eliminating redundant staff positions and sharing resources. I was asked to comment on this plan. During the course of the study, I found that not only two separate divisions but also two separate cultures existed in conflict in research administration in addition to many subcultures within each distinctive group. One group had a client-representative (or client-centered) approach to serving faculty. When a faculty member asked his or her client representative about a problem, the representative would find the answer. Instead of sending the faculty member round-robin to seek the answer from other administrators, the representative would find the information from a colleague in administration if unable to answer the question. Thus, the faculty member typically dealt with only one person. This group was a cohesive team, substituting for one another as necessary. The faculty was very pleased with this division's performance.

The second team was organized according to function, ranging from accounting to a sponsored projects office. In general, most staff members in this division were isolated or buffered from faculty. Their interactions were primarily with faculty secretaries and administrative assistants. This division was rife with territories and factions. The division's most notable subcultures were the old guard and the new guard. The old guard believed that the existing system had worked for many years and wanted to maintain it. The new guard expressed a desire to experiment with new systems, including computerizing many functions. The faculty was not satisfied with this division's performance. Faculty members with questions would have to know the right person to call or make several calls to find the right person for the function. Moreover, the warring factions often prevented any work from taking place because people on various sides would not talk to each other.

Both divisions were aware of the merger potential. Because of a long-standing animosity between the two divisions, neither wanted the merger. The client-representative service group feared losing its tightly knit social organization. This division's faculty members feared losing the group's excellent service. Staff in the second division did not want a client-representative approach. They were accustomed to working within a specific function without any knowledge of their peers' activities. From their perspective, the functional approach was as effective as the client-representative approach.

When the director and the dean asked me to comment on the proposed plan to consolidate research administration, I explained that research administration stood at an organizational crossroads. Many organizational configurations were possible to improve overall performance. Merging the two divisions, however, was not a solution. Although the merger seemed logical, it would not be productive. Combining the divisions would escalate existing culture conflict and significantly reduce overall efficiency. Mixing the client-representative group with the function-oriented division would rip the social fabric of the groups apart and diminish their capacity to serve faculty. Similarly, the imposition of the client-representative approach on the function-oriented group would catalyze conflict. The function-oriented group would interpret collaboration as territorial invasion, prying, or even spying.

My recommendation was not to merge the two units, regardless of the short-term financial benefits. Instead, I suggested that the client-representative division remain untouched. The function-oriented group needed to know that its social organization was respected, but it also needed assistance in reducing internal strife and developing smoother contact with clients. Both groups agreed with my descriptions and recommendations. The overall ethnographic description of research administration convinced the dean to make the counterintuitive decision not to merge the divisions.

This counterintuitive conclusion or crystallization derived from a detailed study of each culture and its various subcultures. The emic perspective helped to put the entire picture together in my formal etic or social scientific role (see also Fetterman, 1981b, for other case examples.)

Analysis has no single form or stage in ethnography. Multiple analyses and forms of analyses are essential. Analysis takes place throughout any ethnographic endeavor, from the selection of the problem to the final stages of writing. Analysis is iterative and often cyclical in ethnography (Goetz & LeCompte, 1984; Hammersley & Atkinson, 1983; Taylor & Bogdan, 1984). The researcher builds a firm knowledge base in bits and pieces, asking questions, listening, probing, comparing and contrasting, synthesizing, and evaluating information. The ethnographer must run sophisticated tests on data long before leaving the field. A formal, identifiable stage of analysis, however, does take place when the ethnographer physically leaves the field. Half the analysis at this stage involves additional triangulation, sifting for patterns, developing new matrices, and applying statistical tests to the data. The other half takes place during the final stages of writing an ethnography or an ethnographically informed report.

6

Recording the Miracle: Writing

*The difference between the right word
and the nearly right word is the same as
that between lightning and the lightning bug.*

—Mark Twain

Writing is hard work. Writing well is even harder. Ethnography requires good writing skills at every stage. Research proposals, field notes, memoranda, interim reports, final reports, articles, and books are the tangible products of ethnographic work. The ethnographer can share these written works with participants to verify their accuracy and with colleagues for review and consideration. Ethnography offers many intangibles through the media of participation and verbal communication. Written products, however, unlike ephemeral conversations and interactions, withstand the test of time.

Ethnographic writing is as difficult and as satisfying as descriptions of nature. From simple notes about small events, special landmarks, or even the temperature to efforts to describe an experience or explain a sudden insight, ethnographic writing requires an eye for detail, an ability to express that detail in its proper context, and the language skills to weave small details and bits of meaning into a textured fabric. The ethnographer must re-create the varied forms of social organization and interaction that months of observation and study have revealed. The manifold symbolism every culture displays and the adaptiveness of people to their environment must somehow come to life on the page.

Ethnographic writing comes in a variety of styles, from clear and simple to byzantine. Many ethnographers model their efforts after those of an author they admire. They adapt their model to suit various subjective and objective considerations: tone, context, message, time constraints, purpose, and so on. As a result, each writer develops a literary voice that becomes clearer and more individual with experience. All ethnographers, however—regardless of how well developed their style—need to adapt their writing to suit their particular and varying audiences. As is the case with every writer, the ethnographer's ability to write to different audiences will determine the effectiveness of the work.

Writing good field notes is very different from writing a solid and illuminating ethnography or ethnographically informed report. Note taking is the rawest kind of writing. The note taker typically has an audience of one. Thus, although clarity, concision, and completeness are vital in note taking, style is not a primary consideration.

Writing for an audience, however, means writing to that audience. Reports for academics, government bureaucrats, private and public industry officials, medical professionals, and various educational program sponsors require different formats, languages, and levels of abstraction. The brevity and emphasis on findings in a report written for a program-level audience might raise some academics' eyebrows and cause them to question the project's intellectual level. Similarly, a refereed scholarly publication would frustrate program personnel, who would likely feel that the researcher is wasting their time—time that they need to take care of business—with irrelevant concerns. In essence, both parties feel that the researcher is simply not in touch with their reality. These two audiences are both interested in the fieldwork and the researcher's conclusions but have different needs and concerns. Good ethnographic work can usually produce information that is relevant to both parties. The skillful ethnographer will communicate effectively with all audiences—using the right smoke signals for the right tribe. (See Fetterman, 1987b, for a discussion of the ethnographer as rhetorician; see also Yin, 1984, for a discussion of differing audiences in the presentation of a case study.)

Writing is part of the analysis process as well as a means of communication (Hammersley & Atkinson, 1983). Writing clarifies thinking. In sitting down to put thoughts on paper, an individual must organize those thoughts and sort out the specific ideas and relationships. Writing often reveals gaps in knowledge. If the researcher is still in the field when those gaps are discovered, additional interviews and observations of specific settings are necessary. If the researcher has left the field, field notes and telephone calls must suffice. Embryonic ideas often come to maturity during writing, as the ethnographer crystallizes months of thought.

From conception—as a twinkle in the ethnographer's eye—to delivery in the final report, an ethnographic study progresses through written stages. A brief review of some of the milestones in the ethnographic life cycle highlights the significance of writing in ethnography.

RESEARCH PROPOSALS

The ethnographer's ideas have their first expression in the research proposal. Sponsors judge the quality of the design, the significance of the problem, the methodology, including analysis, and the budget—all of which must be communicated in writing. The magnitude of a specific problem and the sophistication of research tools can be described in myriad ways. Only a few approaches, however, will compete favorably with other deserving proposals. Sponsors are a very special audience. Each sponsor has idiosyncratic standards, requirements, criteria, interests, and funding capabilities. The ethnographer's ability to communicate with sponsors will directly affect the success, shape, and tone of the research endeavor—or whether the endeavor is even undertaken.

Careful and deliberate writing can ensure an appropriate match between sponsor and researcher. Like an employment interview, the proposal is the first communication between individuals who must decide quickly whether they can work together; if so, they must learn to do so. A well-drafted proposal can chart the way for both the researcher and the sponsor. Clear, direct statements—free of circumlocutions, jargon, qualifying clauses, and vague, passive phrasing—can communicate the ideas, how the study will carry them out, and who will conduct the work and for how much and how long. Shared understandings and values reduce misunderstandings, miscommunications, and consequent tensions. Ambiguity invites misunderstanding and turmoil. Lack of clarity may also indicate to the sponsor that the ethnographer's thinking is fuzzy. Writing is thus both an exercise in clarifying thoughts and plans and a form of self-presentation.

Planning and foresight are essential in ethnographic research. The more organized the effort, the smoother its progress. The proposal's language and structure reflect the writer's organization. Committing plans to writing identifies gaps in scheduling and thinking. In addition, proper planning during the proposal stage can ensure that enough time and money are available for important aspects of the research effort. Improper planning can result in terminating a project before it has addressed all the salient issues. It can also result in research that follows an aimless pattern, like a ship adrift, wasting time and effort. After the proposal is accepted and the work funded, and after the carefully crafted letters necessary to gain entry to the community have been written, the next significant writing challenge lies in taking good field notes.

FIELD NOTES

Field notes are the brick and mortar of an ethnographic edifice. These notes consist primarily of data from interviews and daily observation. They form an early stage of analysis during data collection and contain the raw data necessary for later, more elaborate analyses. Many field note guidelines and techniques are available to assist ethnographers. The most important rule, however, is to write the information down.

Fieldwork inundates the ethnographer with information, ideas, and events. Ethnographic work is exhausting, and the fieldworker will be tempted to stop taking notes or to postpone typing the day's hieroglyphics each night. Memory fades quickly, however, and unrecorded information will soon be overshadowed by subsequent events. Too long a delay sacrifices the rich immediacy of concurrent notes.

Shorthand, Symbols, and Mnemonics

Ethnographers use numerous techniques to improve their accuracy in recording events in the field. For example, they learn a highly personalized shorthand for recording interviews. Short phrases or key words represent an event, an image, or parts of a conversation. Standard abbreviations and symbols are common aids in note taking: ♀, ♂, +, $, and so on. Question marks and exclamation points are useful notations, reminding the ethnographer of a finding or another unanswered question. These devices enable the ethnographer to take extensive notes during the day, capturing both depth and breadth. Ideally, the translation of these notes takes place immediately after the interview or observation while the memory is sharp. Routine end-of-day translation, however, is more usual and more practical in many cases. These abbreviations and symbols are written snapshots or mnemonic devices. They trigger the memory, carrying a rush of images to the brain and enabling the ethnographer to reconstruct entire episodes.

Reconstruction

Note taking is inappropriate in some situations—for example, funerals, fights, and certain religious festivals. Field notes are still important but taking them is more difficult. In this case, a complete reconstruction is necessary. In his study of tramps, Spradley (1970) ran to the lavatory after almost every interview with drunks to transcribe events. Many of his interviewees thought that he had a bladder problem. Powdermaker (1966) sat in her car for hours writing up sensitive conversations. Recalling long passages of conversation accurately requires practice. Like bards who memorized thousands of lines of song, however, ethnographers can accurately recall vast amounts of data with training and experience. Unlike the bards, however, the ethnographer must write down this information as quickly as possible before absorbing new material.

FIELD NOTE
ORGANIZATION

Keeping field notes organized and cross-referenced can facilitate formal stages of analysis, from preliminary hypothesis testing in the field to the final writing. Notes can be organized by topic in a loose-leaf folder as easily as they can in a computer database. The database approach greatly facilitates analysis, as was discussed in Chapters 4 and 5, and reduces the time needed to write an ethnography. (See Wolcott, 1975, concerning the amount of time typically required to write an ethnography; see also Levine, 1985, for a discussion of organizational strategies—specifically, the principles of data storage and retrieval.)

Speculations, cues, lists, and personal diary-type comments should remain in a separate category from observation notes. Such notes are working documents that help guide the ethnographer's work. They serve as a reminder to follow up on a long list of topics and tasks. Written on the back of an envelope or on a computer with an automatic reminder program, these notes also document part of the ethnographic process. Using them, the ethnographer can retrace steps to identify the strategy that helped to uncover a specific layer of meaning during the research. A personal diary can be both an effective coping strategy during particularly difficult and dangerous fieldwork and a means of quality control. Notes about the researcher's mood, attitude, and judgments during a specific stage of the research endeavor can provide a context from which to view primary field notes at that stage. Maintaining these separate files thus becomes a quality control on data collection and analysis. (See Schwandt & Halpern, 1988, concerning auditing field notes; see also Bogdan & Biklen, 1982, for an additional discussion of writing field notes.)

BOX 6.1
Organization of Field Notes

A variety of useful ways of organizing field notes are available. I have found that one approach in particular ensures an efficient and effective fieldwork experience and, in the process, greatly facilitates the process of writing.

Field notes can be organized in a looseleaf folder, with tabs to identify each section. The first section consists of a running index, which can be used to help find specific topic areas or passages. The second section consists of the proposal or contract. The third section holds the time and budget records necessary to administer the effort properly. The fourth section holds all correspondence, and the fifth section contains preliminary notes used during the early survey phase of the research effort. (Field notes in this section of the notebook are used to develop the proposal and to delimit further the ethnographer's scope during the early stages of fieldwork.) The remaining sections are all subsets of the proposal. The proposal identifies the major categories for study, with each section containing a research topic.

The first page of each section is a cover sheet containing purpose, methods, findings, conclusions, and recommendations. This system compels the ethnographer to clarify the purpose of the task, accurately record the specific methods in use to explore the topic, and summarize findings and conclusions. In addition, this organizational aid provides a convenient reference throughout the study for recommended future courses of action. The cover sheet also enables the ethnographer to generate memoranda or other summary communications to share with colleagues, sponsors, and people in the field. The memoranda in turn—together with participant responses—generate the report or ethnography.

The findings section of the cover sheet is cross-referenced to the specific field notes, photographs, and tape recordings or transcripts that document each finding. For example, the field notes of an interview represent the raw data. The interview notes might be accompanied by observational records, matrices, and pictures used to triangulate the information. These documents or raw data refer back to the summary sheet for convenience. (The same set of observational notes or interview data can be used to support a number of findings in other sections of the folder or work papers.)

The ethnographer can develop new topics that emerge from an initial investigation of the proposal topics or subsets of existing ones. A computer can maintain and organize many of these records, as discussed in Chapter 4. In many cases, however, hard copy, as well as photographic records, is essential. This approach to field note organization reminds the ethnographer of the study's purpose and direction; allows the fieldworker easy access to preliminary findings, conclusions, and recommendations; and enables others to review the research effort.

MEMORANDA

Ethnographers produce summaries of the research effort during various stages of their work. This synthesizing tool helps them gauge progress. In my work in higher education, I find brief memoranda useful in consolidating my understanding of a situation. I share them with the people I am working with and ask for feedback. This interaction places a check on my perceptions before I use them as a basis for understanding the next stage or development. In addition, memoranda provide participants with an opportunity to share in the research process. Writing memoranda throughout a study also makes report writing much easier. The ethnographer can draw introductory and background sections from the proposal that was modified after field experience. The core of the report then comes directly from the memoranda and feedback generated throughout the study. Thus, the ethnographer needs only to finish the final synthesis, which explains how all the memoranda and the responses fit together. Participants should have no significant surprises at the end of the process.

INTERIM REPORTS

In contract research work, interim reports are more common than memoranda. These reports are preliminary summaries of the ethnographer's knowledge at prespecified intervals during the study. These reports go to sponsors, participants, and colleagues for review. In testing an ethnographer's understanding of the program or culture and allowing specific feedback for each aspect of the report, interim reports are an invaluable contribution to the quality of the research effort.

FINAL REPORTS, ARTICLES, AND BOOKS

The last stage in ethnographic research is writing the final report, article, or book. These final products often represent the ethnographer's last opportunity to present a refined, analyzed picture of the culture under study. These three forms of highly crystallized expression require the same foundation of data, hard work, and insight as do the other forms of writing but differ in tone, style, format, distribution, and economic value in the marketplace.

The variety of reports, articles, and books is so great that in one chapter I can do little more than discuss a few generic characteristics and guidelines for each type. A brief review of the most common forms of ethnographic publishing is essential, however, because sharing knowledge, which usually involves publishing findings, is a critical part of an ethnographer's work. Publishing is an ethnographer's way of sharing observations and conclusions and then learning from the feedback generated by the published material.

A government report is typically more pragmatic than an article or book. It is likely to have an immediate impact on the program or group under study. Typically, the ethnographer focuses on a specific policy issue in the report. The language is likely to be bureaucratese full of abstract jargon (words such as prioritization and implementation)—a must for communicating effectively with government agencies. The report may contain a technical and a nontechnical compilation of the findings. It will typically have an executive summary for policymakers who do not have the time or inclination to read the entire report. Advisory panels—composed of academics, practitioners, and government commissioners—maintain quality control on the effort and the product. In many cases, the panels play a direct role in negotiating the wording of key passages.

An article is a cross section or a highly condensed version of the ethnographer's overall effort. It often discusses a specific issue in-depth. The author typically will briefly indicate how the work contributes to knowledge development, theory, or methodology. The audience usually consists of academic colleagues, who have a direct impact on the shape of the author's work in refereed journals because they recommend publication or rejection. They also recommend specific revisions. The author must respond to such suggestions before the article is accepted for publication. Collegial influence can have a dramatic effect on the final product—refining and improving it or forcing the author to make an inappropriate detour (for more about writing journal articles, see Bogdan & Biklen, 1982, pp. 183-190; Van Til, 1987).

The greater length of a book compared to an article provides the ethnographer with more latitude. The audience, once again, is composed primarily of academic colleagues. The structure of ethnographic manuscripts varies, but an ethnography typically discusses fundamental elements about the culture, such as its structure and organization, history, politics, religion, economy, and worldview. A specific theme that emerged during the ethnography might become the focal point of discussion throughout the text. This theme might be a critical feature of the culture, its ethos, or the manner in which members adapt or fail to adapt to their environment. On receipt of a manuscript, the publisher requests reviews from appropriate colleagues in the field to help make a go/no-go decision. The reviews can determine the fate of the manuscript as well as its tone or emphasis. Authors can seek out other publishers or journals if their work is rejected or if they disagree with the recommended changes. Some publishers and journals are so prized in the field, however, that the author has no realistic alternative. (See Powell, 1985, for a discussion about the decision-making process in scholarly publishing.)

In addition to disciplinary and status differences among reports, articles, and books, differences exist in subtopic focus and in whether the orientation is basic or applied. Whatever the work, the ethnographer must select the most appropriate audience to write—the readers on whom the work will have an impact and who will judge it appropriately. Once the ethnographer has determined the appropriate audience, he or she then must gear the writing style to that audience.

Reports usually have limited circulation, targeting sponsors, various government agencies, program personnel, and some academic colleagues. Reports may or may not be copyrighted and generally do not generate royalties; they are products that are delivered and paid for as part of a research project. Report deadlines are a double-edged sword. They ensure a timely response to specific policy questions but preclude careful attention to style.

The circulation of articles depends on the journal in which they appear. An ethnographer interested in reaching the largest possible audience within the general boundaries of the topic will attempt to publish in a scholarly journal with a large circulation. If the aim is simply to share knowledge with a very small, specialized group of scholars, highly specific journals are the best choice. In both instances, the ethnographer makes trade-offs in terms of exposure and impact or influence. Refereed journals are more highly respected and prestigious than nonrefereed journals because they have built-in quality control and publishing in them is more difficult. Journal articles are usually copyrighted. The journal holds the copyright, but the authors generally have the right to use the article in any book or collection they author or edit. Journal articles do not produce any royalties unless they are reprinted in a book. Such articles are less timely than reports but more timely than books. Manuscript review for a journal article often takes from 2 to 8 months or more. Revisions, galley proofing, and general production time may delay publication another 2 to 6 months. For this reason, many high-energy physicists prefer on-line electronic articles to traditionally published articles—they need to keep up with rapid changes in their field.

Internet publishing represents an alternative to printed publications. Some estimates put the number of online scholarly journals at over 500 (see http://ejournals.cic.net). As this paragraph was being written, Nicholas Burbules and Gene Glass announced the creation of an online journal of book reviews in education (http://www.ed.asu.edu/edrev). Refereed on-line journals, such as *Cultural Dynamics* (http://dynamics.rug.ac.be/home.html), *Education Policy Analysis Archives* (http://olam.ed.asu.edu/epaa/), *Journal of World Anthropology* (gopher://wings.buffalo.edu:70/h0/academic/department/anthropology/jwa/index), *Journal of World Systems* (http://csf.colorado.edu/wsystems/jwsr.html), and *Qualitative Report* (http://www.nova.edu/ssss/QR/index.html), represent an emerging and exciting vehicle for sharing ethnographic insights and findings in real time. Articles can be reviewed by a larger number of colleagues in a much shorter period of time using e-mail. In addition, articles can be published electronically much quicker than they can in traditional media. Colleagues can critique these electronically published pieces more rapidly, which allows authors to revise their work in less time than it would take to publish an original document traditionally. Moreover, the cost of electronic publication allows journals to be accessed without cost to readers. This medium also allows for authors to publish their raw data, including their interviews, linked to the same "page"; this allows the readers to analyze the data immediately for themselves and sort the same data in other ways depending on their own theoretical orientation. Glass's (1997) electronic journal article about school choice provides an illustration. She links her interviews directly to her table of contents (Figures 6.1 and 6.2; see also the article at http://olam.ed.asu.edu/epaa/v5n1.html).

Some colleagues and publishers are concerned about copyright issues. Norms are developing in this area, however, and publishing conventions are being successfully applied to this medium (Burbules & Bruce, 1995). I have published articles on the Internet and one of my recent books, *Empowerment Evaluation: Knowledge and Tools for Self-Assessment and Accountability* (Fetterman, Kaftarian, & Wandersman, 1996), was distributed both in traditional print format and over the Internet. I have not experienced any abuse of privilege in this area. I have, however, experienced a rapid and exponentially expanded distribution of ideas.

Scholarly books are more difficult to write than articles—a result in part of their greater length and in part of the larger scope of intellectual effort that is required. Stamina and concentration are essential: An article requires tremendous effort to reduce mountains of data and pools of analysis into concise expression. A book requires the same effort multiplied many times. In addition, a book is the ultimate scholarly format and will be judged by generation after generation of readers.

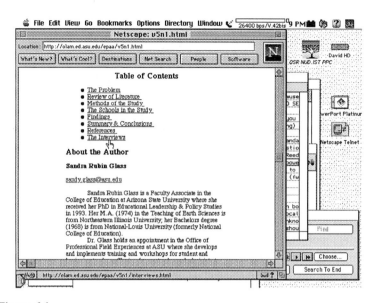

Figure 6.1.
SOURCE: Reproduced with permission from S. Glass and G. Glass.

Books—unlike most articles—are reviewed publicly (for examples, see Fetterman, 1986c, 1986d). Although most reviewers try to give an honest critique of the work (Janesick, 1986), a poor match between reviewer and text can be disastrous. Almost all reviewers look for errors, sins of omission, and conceptual flaws in a text. Some have the wisdom to judge a book on its own merits; others judge it against an ideal but unrelated model (for additional discussion on this topic, as well as a case example, see Bank, 1986; Fetterman, 1986a). In some cases, the publisher selects a reviewer precisely because his or her view of the topic is completely different from that of the author. Colleagues familiar with the players learn how to interpret reviewer comments and can learn much from this exercise. Although review comments must sometimes be taken with a grain of salt, the review process—with all its faults—appears to be the best system available.

How widely books circulate depends on the publisher. Some publishers have highly integrated dissemination systems, including databases of professional association membership lists, classified according to interest and topic area. Such systems enable publishers to identify their market and target their advertising. The author has a direct interest in this process because the author of a book typically receives royalties. The publisher owns the copyright—to prevent competition from that same author—and the author retains limited publication rights.

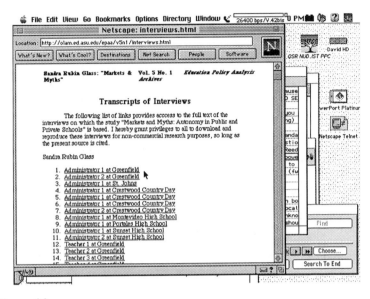

Figure 6.2.
SOURCE: Reproduced with permission from S. Glass and G. Glass.

A book is usually an ethnographer's least timely published effort. Some ethnographies are written many years after the fieldwork. Once a publisher accepts a manuscript, actual publication may take an additional year or two. Exceptions do exist. Some publishers now request camera-ready copy of the author's manuscript to expedite the process. Given the typical lag between acceptance and publication, however, authors are fortunate that most scholarly ethnographic books are timeless and have a long shelf life. (See Whyte's *Street Corner Society,* 1955, for a classic example; see also Lareau, 1987, for discussion about the delay in publication of Whyte's text.)

All written ethnographic expressions share some common features. Most important are thick description and verbatim quotations. Use of the ethnographic present and an explicit statement of the role of the ethnographer are also characteristic.

THICK DESCRIPTION AND VERBATIM QUOTATIONS

Thick description and verbatim quotations are the most identifiable features of ethnographic field notes, reports, articles, and books. Ethnographers take great pains to describe a cultural scene or event in tremendous detail. The aim is to convey the feel and the facts of an observed event. Ideally, the ethnographer shares the participant's understanding of the situation with the reader. Thick description is a written record of cultural interpretation. In Chapter 2, the difference between a wink and a blink was discussed. A thin description would simply describe a rapid closing of the eyelid. A thick description gives context, telling the reader whether the movement was a blink caused by a mote in someone's eye or a romantic signal transmitted across a crowded room. Thus, the description would incorporate the cultural meaning and the ethnographer's analysis.

Thick description can portray a variety of cultural scenes and episodes. The following example is from a discussion about ethical dilemmas during fieldwork in the inner city (Fetterman, 1986e):

> On what was to have been the last day of the site visit a student befriended me. After a few hours of conversation about his life and the neighborhood, he decided to show me around. He introduced me to a number of the leaders running life in the streets. It was getting hot and he knew I was from California, so he brought me into a health food store for a cold drink and a snack. We went in and my new friend winked at the owner of the store and told him to give me a granola bar with some natural soda. I said thanks and reached out my hand for the granola bar and felt something else under the bar. It was a nickel bag of marijuana. I looked at the owner, then I looked at my friend. I did not want to show any form of disapproval or ingratitude, but this was not exactly what I had in mind when I agreed to play the role of guest, visitor, and friend.
>
> A moment later, I heard steps in perfect stride. I looked over to the front window and saw two policemen walking by, looking right in the window. My hand was still in the air with the mixed contents for all to see. My heart dropped to the floor. My first thought was, "I'm going to get busted. How am I going to explain this to my colleagues at the research corporation?"
>
> Fortunately, the police disappeared as quickly as they had appeared. I asked my friend what had just transpired. He explained to me that the police were paid off regularly and would bother you only if they needed money or if an owner had not made a contribution. (pp. 27-28)

Thick descriptions start out as long, unwieldy, redundant entities in note form during fieldwork. The author must carefully select and prune these notes to illustrate a point or present an interpretation in a report or book. Ethnographic writing is a process of compression as the ethnographer moves from field notes to written text. The goal is to represent reality concisely but completely and not to reproduce every detail and word. A complete reproduction is not possible or desirable: It is not science, and no one will take the time to read it all.

Verbatim quotations are also a sine qua non of ethnography. They are a permanent record of a person's thoughts and feelings. Verbatim quotations convey the fear, anger, frustration, exhilaration, and joy of a human being and contain surface and deep, embedded meanings about the person's life. They can present a host of ideas to the reader: basic "factual" data, social and economic indicators, and internal consistency or patterned inconsistencies. The reader can infer the values and worldview of the speaker from these passages. Long verbatim quotations help convey a sense of immediacy to the reader. In addition, judicious use of such raw data in reports and ethnographies can provide the reader with sufficient data to determine whether the ethnographer's interpretations and conclusions are warranted.

During the study of the drop-out program, I learned about the practice of arson for hire in the community from a young mother who lived in the neighborhood. Her words conveyed a vivid picture of this crime (Fetterman, 1983). Corina said that she

> Woke up to a phone call at two in the morning. The man over the phone said to be out of the house in 15 minutes because it was going to burn. That's what they do when it's arson, they call you just like that at two in the morning. I had my rollers on and I was in my bathrobe, that's all I had. I was on the second floor and my grandma she was on the third. I can still remember seein' the flames all around her in her wheelchair. I tried to get her out but I couldn't. I had rheumatic fever you know, so I'm weak. She was so heavy I just couldn't. I got my babies out but she was so heavy. I just watched her die. I still go to the county [psychiatrist] even now. I dream about it. It still frightens me. I couldn't save her. (p. 218)

The dimensions of Corina's personal tragedy and the personal nature of this crime would have been lost in a third-person description. Her own words provide a concise, accurate, and personal description of the effects of arson for hire in the community. Thick description and verbatim quotations have tremendous face validity in ethnography (see Ryles as cited in Geertz, 1973).

ETHNOGRAPHIC PRESENT

Ethnographies are usually written in the ethnographic present. The ethnographic present is a slice of life—a motionless image. This literary illusion suggests that the culture stands still through time—even after the

time that the ethnography describes. Ethnographers are keenly aware of
change in sociocultural systems. They often focus on change in a program,
a culture, or any group. Fieldwork may have taken years, but the ethnographer writes about the events as if they were occurring in the present. This
convention is partly a matter of linguistic convenience. It is also a way to
maintain consistency in description and to keep the story alive, however.
Fundamentally, the ethnographer uses the present tense because fieldwork—which could continue indefinitely—must end at some arbitrary
point. Fieldwork is never done; it is just terminated. Time and other
resources are not inexhaustible, and natives tire of being observed. The
ethnographer realizes that no matter how long the study, the culture will
change the moment the fieldwork ends. The best the ethnographer can do
is to describe the culture as accurately as possible up to the point of
departure. Ideally, the ethnographic present is true to the ethnographer's
image of the culture at the time of the study.

ETHNOGRAPHIC PRESENCE

   Ethnographers attempt to be unobtrusive and to reduce their influence
on the natural situation. Their purpose is to describe another culture as it
operates naturally. Ethnographers are honest, however. They recognize that
their presence is a factor in this human equation. Thus, rather than present
an artificial picture, ethnographers openly describe their roles in events
during fieldwork. The ethnographic presence tells the reader how close the
ethnographer is to the people and to the data. The technique can contribute
additional credibility to the researcher's findings. These embedded self-
portraits simultaneously serve as a quality control, documenting the degree
of contamination or influence the ethnographer has on the people under
study.
   At the same time, the ethnographer should not dominate the setting, nor
should the ethnographer's signature be in every word or on every page. The
researcher need not include every parenthetical thought to demonstrate
intellectual prowess. In describing a culture, the focus of the writing should
be on the topic. Alfred Hitchcock's signature—appearing on screen for a
few seconds in each of his movies—is an example of an explicit presence.
His style, particularly his use of camera angles, is an example of implicit
presence. Ethnographers leave both explicit and implicit signatures on their
work. Some are subtle, and others are as bold as van Gogh's brush strokes

in his *Cornfield With Crows*. An artfully crafted ethnographic presence can convey the depth and breadth of the ethnographer's experience in the field.

ETHNOGRAPHICALLY INFORMED REPORTS

Ethnographers do not always have the luxury of completing a full-blown ethnography. Instead, they must write ethnographically informed reports or other efforts. An ethnographically informed report may require the same effort as an ethnography, or it may approximate the effort by applying some ethnographic concepts and techniques to research. In either case, the report has the flavor of an ethnography, but its structure and format resemble those of publications funded by a public- or private-sector sponsor. An ethnographically informed report is as useful as a full-blown ethnography to the right audience. Ethnographically informed reports that only approximate the effort a traditional ethnography requires, however, will not be as credible because the writer loses many built-in quality controls when ethnographic concepts and methods are not integrated.

LITERATURE

Literary artists are keen observers of the human drama. They have created classic stories and characters representing fundamental values and social relationships. Literary works can be useful to the ethnographer at various stages in the work. During fieldwork, the events of everyday life often parallel the plots of masterpieces. These parallels can help to unravel the complex performances that the ethnographer attends.

Literature is probably most useful, however, as a tool to help ethnographers communicate their insights. A number of literary conventions and writing techniques are available for the ethnographer to use. The author may assume the voice of different speakers or may appear omniscient or transparent. The author can expand or contract through narrative pace. Use of concrete metaphors, rich similes, parallelism, irony, and many other devices on a larger plane convey the true feel, taste, and smell of a moment.

Ethnographers use this wordcraft to make their science meaningful and effective. I used Shakespeare's resonant phrase "a comedy of errors" in my "Blaming the Victim" article about the drop-out program (Fetterman, 1981b). The phrase aptly characterized in a concise and instantly comprehensible fashion the misuse of the treatment-control design and the federal bureaucratic intervention in the study. The phrase—as a description of the behavior of educational agencies and researchers in a national research effort—conveys the absurdity of the experience and its tragedy (misevaluation). Henrik Ibsen's play *An Enemy of the People* provided a powerful image that accurately reflected my experience in attempting to publish my research findings about the misapplication of the treatment-control design in the drop-out study. In this story, Dr. Stockmann, the play's protagonist and a medical official, attempts to publish his discovery of contaminants in the town's famous baths. He encounters significant resistance from the townspeople, who derive their income from tourists frequenting the baths. I used this poignant story to convey my own frustration; it captured the emotional tension and outrage I experienced in the face of harsh resistance to a public discussion of the misuse of a paradigm fundamental to educational research (Fetterman, 1982b). Writing about art can also be an effective way to communicate. In the same article, I used art to illustrate a conceptual point and to abstract the situation from the reader and the observer—like Dali's painting of Dali painting Dali painting, ad infinitum.

REVISING AND EDITING

The last stages of writing always include revising and editing. Writing is both mechanical and artistic. Paragraphs must be shifted to fit in the right organizational or conceptual sequence. Sentences should be grammatical. Participles should not dangle, and citations should correspond to references. Phrases must be carefully crafted to capture the imagination of the reader and yet remain scientific. Examples must be compelling and precise. Titles must catch the reader's eye and remain honest. The author must polish all these facets of the work in addition to making sure the work is cogent, conceptually coherent, and comprehensive but concise. All these tasks take time. (For useful writing guides, as a primer see Bernstein, 1965, 1977; Strunk & White, 1959; see Barzun, 1984, for a excellent graduate text.)

Proper organization can reduce the time necessary to write drafts of ethnographic products, but revising and polishing take additional time and a tremendous amount of effort. The amount of time depends on the quality of the first draft, the writer's talent, and the amount of time available. Time should also be allocated for review by critical friends and colleagues.

Attention to detail, including proofing galleys, is important. The absence of a single word or letter can inadvertently change meanings. Passages supporting a complex argument can be lost between copyediting and galley stages. Without sufficient attention to the role of editing manuscripts, opportunities for last-minute updates can be lost. Time devoted to these tasks is always time well spent.

7

Walking Softly Through the Wilderness: Ethics

Take only pictures, leave only footprints.

—Adapted from the National
Speleological Society

Ethnographers do not work in a vacuum, they work with people. They often pry into people's innermost secrets, sacred rites, achievements, and failures. In pursuing this personal science, ethnographers subscribe to a code of ethics that preserves the participants' rights, facilitates communication in the field, and leaves the door open for further research.

This code specifies first and foremost that the ethnographer do no harm to people or the community under study. In seeking a logical path through the cultural wilds, the ethnographer is careful not to trample the feelings of natives or desecrate what the culture calls sacred. This respect for social environment ensures not only the rights of the people but also the integrity of the data and a productive, enduring relationship between the people and the researcher. Professionalism and a delicate step demonstrate the ethnographer's deep respect, admiration, and appreciation for the people's way of life. Noninvasive ethnography is not only good ethics but also good science (see the American Anthropological Association's "Principles of Professional Responsibility"; see also Rynkiewich & Spradley, 1976; Weaver, 1973).

This chapter will briefly discuss the diversity of ethnographic approaches to illustrate the complexity of ethical decision making in ethnography. It will then locate these moments of decision within the life cycle of the ethnographic research project.

THE ETHNOGRAPHER'S ROLE

The role a researcher assumes to explore a culture or a specific problem within it determines how a problem is defined. For example, psychologists, anthropologists, physicians, and politicians will define the same problem in radically different ways. Similarly, different types of ethnographers will define problems differently and approach them in very different ways. Throughout, this book has abstracted basic features of ethnography common to most ethnographic approaches, noting exceptions as necessary. Here, the focus is on how the adoption of a specific ethnographic role—whether academic (basic) or applied—influences every stage of the research project, from defining the problem to reporting findings.

ACADEMIC AND APPLIED ETHNOGRAPHY

Academic ethnography typically takes place within the academy to enlighten students and colleagues and to build a knowledge base about a culture or theory. Academic or basic research is the dominant mode of investigation. Applied research, however, also occurs within this domain.

Applied research usually aims at social change and often at influencing institutional policy. Most applied ethnographic work—administrative, action, and advocate ethnography—takes place in schools, hospitals, government agencies, and other organizational settings outside of academe (Spradley & McCurdy, 1975). Each approach has an important role to play in the development of knowledge and action. Ethnographers select the approach that best suits them personally and professionally, and each approach is ethical and productive in the appropriate setting. Each approach, however, can also pose ethical dilemmas and constraints. Ethnographic approaches—like technology—are better or worse, ethical or unethical, according to their application.

Academic Ethnographers

A variety of pressures, from peer to sponsor pressures, shape academic ethnographers. Academic ethnographers feel the pressure to "fit in" just as does every other professional. The pressures of job performance are very real for academics, including the need for job security (tenure) and the need to earn annual increases in salary and rank in the field. The criteria used in evaluating the success of academic ethnographers, however, differ from those used to evaluate the performance of applied ethnographers. Academic evaluation relies heavily on the number and quality of grants, papers, articles and books, committee contributions, accolades, and teaching. These pressures and needs influence what people study—specifically, how they define the problem and how they tackle it. The dean, chair, and other senior scholars in the field shape a scholar's perception of a problem. A researcher's theoretical posture toward exploring a culture or problem may determine that professional's status and rank in the field. This influence may pose a problem when the dominant mode of inquiry is at odds with the perspective of the ethnographer or participant. Similar pressures arise with funding. To secure funding, the scholar must establish a link between a personal research interest and the sponsor's focus. Given a finite amount of resources, a successful grantsperson learns how to define the investigation and specify the research design to win funding. This task often requires some intellectual dexterity, reshaping the focus of inquiry and substituting one unit of analysis for another in writing for different grants.

Academics must be entrepreneurial, enterprising, and independent in the pursuit of knowledge. Ideally, this knowledge will serve the highest purposes—enhancing individual and social enlightenment, self-awareness, and understanding. The academic, however, can become lost along the way. Scholarly research can become an arcane and antediluvian pursuit.

Relevance is always an issue in the ivory tower. Internal pressures produce much work that the public has labeled out of touch, inbred, and part of a self-perpetuating system. (See Jacoby, 1987, for a fascinating discussion on this topic.) The relevance of scholarly efforts must always come under question. Every research effort must have some bearing on the development of knowledge and in some way contribute to the social good.

Habermas's (1968, p. 314) conclusion that "knowledge and interest are one" compels researchers to ask why and for whom they are conducting research. Everyone has a vested interest in the outcomes of a particular research endeavor. Researchers need to be aware of their own vested interests and their role in relation to the maelstrom of vested interests operating in any given study. This issue should not paralyze a researcher, but it should influence the research design and serve as a check on conclusions.

Academic ethnographers conduct their research in the most scholarly and ethical manner possible, as do most researchers. Real-world constraints, however, do affect their research. The myth of the ivory tower has led many to believe that academic anthropologists are immune from outside influences. In fact, they are no more or less immune than are applied ethnographers from the influence and constraints of vested interests.

Applied Ethnographers

The ethical dilemmas that applied ethnographers confront grow out of the context in which they work. A discussion about a few of the most significant types of applied ethnographers provides some clues about the type of ethical decisions each must make. The key to understanding the differences between ethnographic approaches lies in understanding the degree of control the ethnographer has over the design (means) and the implementation (ends) of the study.

Administrative Ethnographers

Administrative ethnographers have control over the means—not the ends—of their efforts. These ethnographers may conduct the research, but administrators design and implement the program or innovation. Much of my own ethnographic evaluation work falls into this category (Fetterman, 1984; Fetterman & Pitman, 1986). For example, in the dropout study I conducted the research, but three other agencies were responsible for operating the program, modifying it according to the research findings, and providing funding. A multitude of vested interests pull at the administrative ethnographer, including the demands of students, teachers, parents, school administrators, local school agencies, program disseminators, sponsors, and the average taxpayer.

Traditional anthropological training prepares ethnographers for handling a variety of conflicting worldviews in research but not for solving the convoluted and tortuous ethical dilemmas that emerge from this context. For example, a classic dilemma for administrative ethnographers involves the reporting of findings. Traditional training states that ethnographers must share their research with all parties involved. In the dropout study, the government contract protocol required that the research report go to the sponsor and to the agency disseminating the programs. At the time the research organization signed the contract to study these programs, it had every reason to believe that the disseminating agency was serving the programs' best interests and would share this information with them.

The agency disseminating the programs, however, did not want two of the local dropout programs to have the information. The rationale was that one program was new and might not be capable of interpreting the findings in a constructive and productive manner. The other program was vying with the disseminator for control of the entire operation. This constraint placed us in a difficult position. The research corporation arrived at a creative solution: It delivered the report to the disseminating agency and sponsor, as the contract required. A letter accompanying the report stated that the researcher would request comments directly from each program by the end of the month. The letter also explained that in the event a response was not forthcoming from each program, the researcher would assume that the report had been lost in the mail and would then contact the programs directly—sending them "another" copy of the report. This strategy placed a check on the distribution of drafts without compromising the researcher's role or violating the protocol.

When ethnographers work as management consultants in universities and corporations, the problem is twofold. In this type of setting, the ethnographer writes these reports specifically for a limited audience—senior management. The ethnographer can minimize this ethical dilemma by ensuring that all parties are aware of the report's limited circulation from the outset. Participants always expect implicitly that they will receive at least preliminary feedback, however. The researcher can satisfy this expectation through a telephone call, visit, or memorandum, but rarely can an administrative ethnographer add all participants' names to the distribution list of a final report. In particularly sensitive cases, such as unethical or illegal employee activity, to distribute the findings to anyone other than the employee under investigation and appropriate management personnel would be irresponsible.

Participants often share their organization's basic values. Most employees share a common perception of the company's chain of command for distribution of management information. An unwritten understanding often exists about levels of communication, and thus participants will not expect all information to be public. This attitude also creates a dilemma, making significant disclosures to the "wrong" level inappropriate or taboo from the viewpoint of both management and staff.

As in all branches of research, the fundamental ethical question in ethnographic research is, Who determines the means and ends of the research? In the dropout study, however, this question was a nonquestion because the government was holding all the cards. The project and the study would not exist without government support. Therefore, the ethical question was, Would this study be a useful and productive research endeavor and would it inform the public about a socially significant problem? Part of the answer hinged on whether the government officials were open to the research findings—wherever they led—or had already formed a political conclusion. As an administrative ethnographer, I would have had to decline the opportunity to participate in an effort in which the sponsor had a foregone conclusion; such an exercise would perpetuate a scientific and moral fraud.

Action Ethnographers

Action ethnographers remove themselves from playing a power role as much as possible; they simply conduct the research. The natives design and implement the program or innovation. Sol Tax—the recognized originator and developer of this approach—served the Fox Indians in this capacity (Tax, 1958). He was a catalyst for the Fox: He would clarify issues and list a variety of options or alternatives for change in the community. The decision to implement a specific innovation or goal, such as changing the economic status of the group, remained in the hands of the Fox. They also controlled the means of making this change—for example, making and selling ceramic tiles.

Action ethnography can take place only in a community that is able to determine its fate. Dropouts in the previously discussed study were neither cohesive nor empowered to do anything about their plight, making action ethnography an inappropriate if not impossible approach. In addition, action ethnography requires that the group have a binding decision-making process. Here, too, dropouts could not qualify because they lack any such political system. Finally, action ethnography requires that the group control the resources necessary to make the changes it desires. Dropouts, like the tramps in Spradley's (1970) study, do not control the resources substantive change requires.

Periodically, I have been able to adopt an action ethnography approach in my consulting work. An organization involved in negotiating peaceful resolutions to conflicts between neighbors and between schoolchildren on the playground hired a team of Stanford researchers to help the combatants determine their goals, to describe and evaluate the current status of peacekeeping efforts, and to provide a variety of alternatives to improve and expand these efforts. As principal investigator, I found the effort both satisfying and frustrating. I enjoyed working with the participants and enabling them to make decisions about their fate, and I believed in their work. Watching them choose options that I knew—and had warned them— were fraught with problems and unlikely to work was difficult, however.

Two significant ethical dilemmas emerged from this effort that are generalizable to other action ethnography enterprises. First, the ethnographer must believe that the cause is worthwhile. Helping a group determine its own future is well and good, unless that group has socially destructive or oppressive tendencies. The ethnographer must question the value of the project before contributing to it.

Second, the ethnographer's bias presents a more subtle and pragmatic ethical problem. Presenting a wide variety of options to a group or a client—even options with which the ethnographer may disagree or may dislike—is easy. The ethnographer, however, must somehow control sub-liminal differences in presentation that reflect personal preference. The ethnographer may unintentionally focus on one alternative more than another, spending more time on the preferred choice or presenting it more cogently and convincingly. Information overload is one way—however unintentional—to dissuade people from considering an option. Hundreds of intentional and unintentional tactics are available for influencing a decision while creating the illusion of free choice.

The ethnographer can control this subtle bias once individual prefer-ences become explicit. For example, piloting or testing significant presen-tations on others can help the ethnographer determine that time or verbal emphasis is the same for each topic. The use of partners to share in the presentation and place a check on how each communicates information can reduce subtle but patterned and observable manipulation. Self-discipline and self-criticism are the only tools to control the unconscious influences that will occur in casual conversations with participants.

Advocate Ethnographers

Advocate ethnography is as much a stage in a researcher's life as it is another type of research. Advocate ethnographers allow participants to define their reality, consider their view about the ideal solution to their problems, and then take an active role in making social change happen. These ethnographers serve as advocates for the group. They write in public forums to change public opinion, embarrass power brokers, and provide relevant information about a situation at opportune moments in the policy decision-making forum.

After conducting the dropout study and determining that the programs merited continued funding, I actively disseminated the largely positive findings about the programs to individuals in government and quasi-government institutions. The team of researchers on this project prepared a Joint Dissemination Review Panel Submission substantially based on the ethnographic findings to improve the programs' credibility and potential to secure future funding.

I have also functioned as an advocate ethnographer in academic and government settings. I wrote articles and reports about the misapplication of the treatment-control design in the study about dropouts. I explained that these young individuals were giving society another chance in applying for these programs and then received a slap in the face when they were rejected or placed in the control group. I also suggested that the sponsor's concep-tion of replicating the dropout programs was off target. Programs, like people, adapt to their environment. Expecting a program to replicate itself like a cell is unrealistic and dooms the process to failure before it begins. Both approaches thus blamed the victims—the students and the dropout programs. I wrote and published these articles at a critical point—when efforts were under way to legislate this type of methodology for evaluations of all social programs (Fetterman, 1981b, 1982a, 1982b). Similarly, after conducting extensive research on gifted and talented children in education on state, national, and international levels, I published a book for both the layperson and the professional in the field. The book depicted the plight of gifted and talented children in a system geared toward the mean (Fetterman, 1988a) in an attempt to inform an educated and concerned citizenry about the special needs of gifted children. These actions were in accord with Mills's (1959) position:

> There is no necessity for working social scientists to allow the potential meaning of their work to be shaped by the "accidents" of its setting, or its use to be determined by the purposes of other men. It is quite within their powers to discuss its meanings and decide upon its uses as matters of their own policy. (p. 177)

The presentation of findings to a concerned public is the ethnographer's legitimate responsibility. Such advocacy, however, is a political or public relations activity. The presentation of research findings here aims to influence the use of the information. The researcher who plays politician while conducting and presenting findings is vulnerable to becoming a pawn in the political game. Advocate ethnography is legitimate and ethical but should take place after the research is complete.

RESEARCH LIFE CYCLE

Ethics pervades every stage of ethnographic work. The delicacy ethnographic work requires, however, is nowhere more evident than at the conceptual crossroads where methods and ethical decision making intersect. Ethnographers find themselves at this crossroads when they must make intelligent and informed decisions that satisfy the demands of science and morality.

Inception and Prenatal Care: The Problem

The selection and definition of the culture or subculture and problem, respectively, constitute significant ethical decisions. These decisions inform both inception and prenatal care in the ethnographic life cycle. The decision plants the project's conceptual seeds and nurtures its growth into a fully formed idea and research plan, as discussed in Chapters 1 and 6.

Myriad problems are open to study. Some problems are more significant than others in the larger scheme, and some are value-laden and rife with vested interests. The ethnographer's bias may favor dominant or subordinate interests. For example, in my dropout study, the different groups of people defined the problem in various ways. The differing perspectives derived from their various views of the program. Policymakers were interested in the program as a viable response to serious labor market problems—high dropout rates and high youth unemployment. They were also specifically interested in the transition from school to work. Social reformers, however, considered the program a vehicle to redress historical social inequities and to promote upward social mobility for minority youth. Researchers saw the program as an opportunity to explore equal education opportunity in the United States. The selection and definition of a problem, as well as of the research approach, are ethical statements.

Gestation and Birth: Proposals

The problem, people, and place to study first come together in the proposal to solicit funds for research. Writing a proposal for funding lays the foundation and sets the tone of the study. Experienced ethnographers have learned to take charge during this phase and to establish the budget—to provide for fieldworkers, equipment, and time to think, analyze the data, and write up the findings. Poor planning will have severe repercussions for the health, stability, and longevity of the entire endeavor. Inadequate planning can force an ethnographer to overrun the budget, eliminate important areas of investigation, or initiate closure prematurely, producing a great deal of stress in the process. This stage is also the time to nail down answers to such questions as who is to own the raw data. Typically, ethnographers strive to maintain control of the raw data so that they can maintain confidentiality and protect key informants and other participants from abuses. Specifying ownership of the raw data in the proposal has proved instrumental on more than one occasion in my own research.

Similarly, ethnographers must present their methodological intent to sponsors clearly and honestly. Dishonesty, including significant omissions, will surface later in the study. The period of waiting between writing and submission and acceptance or rejection of the proposal is part of project gestation. Some proposals abort, others are rejected, but the best ones (or at least the most successful proposals) emerge from the process with full funding.

Childhood: Field Preparation

Given a healthy beginning, the ethnographic project enters its formative years—field preparation. Although the proposal presents a detailed blueprint of what the ethnographer plans to do, much work still remains before entering the field. The ethnographer must identify key actors and informants and make detailed schedules, appointments, and other plans to arrange for entrance into the field. In addition, the researcher can mitigate most ethical, methodological, and contractual surprises through regular "checkups" with the sponsor at this stage. During this period, first impressions dominate interactions. The sponsor and program personnel or community members may interpret miscalculations, miscommunications, and protocol violations as ethical faux pas or as outright deceit. These transgressions, conscious or unconscious, real or perceived, can stop an ethnographic study dead in its tracks. The ethnographer therefore must take great care to set the stage for fieldwork.

Adolescence and Adulthood: Fieldwork

Conducting fieldwork is initially like adolescence—for the fieldworker and for the project. The fieldworker must learn a new language, new rituals, and a wealth of new cultural information. This period is marked by tremendous excitement, frustration, and confusion. The ethnographer endures personal and professional turmoil as a part of the learning experience.

A variety of underlying principles cross-cut all forms of ethnographic research and occur at various junctures throughout the ethnographic research life cycle. They come to the fore, however, during the adolescent stage. They range from informed consent to the conduct of a rigorous research effort.

Permission

Ethnographers must formally or informally seek informed consent to conduct their work. In a school district, formal written requests are requisite. Often, the ethnographer's request is accompanied by a detailed account of the purpose and design of the study. Similarly, in most government agencies and private industry, the researcher must submit a formal request and receive written permission. The nature of the request and the consent changes according to the context of the study. For example, no formal structure exists for the researcher to communicate with in a study of tramps. Permission, however, is still necessary to conduct a study. In this situation, the request may be as simple as the following embedded question to a tramp: "I am interested in learning about your life, and I would like to ask you a few questions, if that's all right with you." In this context, a detailed explanation of purpose and method might be counterproductive unless the individual asks for additional detail. Similarly, after receiving initial permission to study a large corporation, the ethnographer must ask each individual for permission to talk about a given topic. Photographs and tape recordings also require the participant's permission. Written permission is particularly important for photographs if the ethnographer plans to use the pictures for educational purposes at professional associations or in speeches and publications. The aim of this standard is to protect the privacy of the individual as directly and simply as possible.

Honesty

Ethnographers must be candid about their task, explaining what they plan to study and how they plan to study it. In some cases, detailed description is appropriate and in others extremely general statements are best, according to the type of audience and the interest in the topic. Few individuals want a detailed discussion of the theoretical and methodological bases of an ethnographer's work. The ethnographer, however, should be ready throughout the study to present this information to any participant who requests it.

Deceptive techniques are unnecessary and inappropriate in ethnographic research. Ethnographers need not disguise their efforts or use elaborate ploys to trick people into responding to a specific stimulus. Other disciplines differ in this respect. Psychology studies, for example, often require that the subject not know the purpose of the experiment.

As a college student, I was a "blind" subject in a psychology replication study of Milgram's experiment on obedience and disobedience to authority. The experiment was simple and ingenious. The researcher told us that the experiment's purpose was to study the effects of punishment on memory. The subjects supposedly played the parts of teacher and student. The "teacher" had to teach the "student" a list of word pairs. The teacher was supposed to shock the student every time the student erred in a response. The first deception, therefore, consisted of misleading the participants about both the purpose of the study and the complicity of the student—who was a supposed blind subject but actually a member of the experiment team.

As the teacher, I sat in a booth facing the student, who was strapped in a chair. The experimenter told me that I had the authority to shock the student every time he produced an unsatisfactory response on a predesigned test. The individual running the experiment said that he took complete responsibility for anything that happened and that I had to participate in the experiment to receive my credits. At that point, I walked out of the experiment. The experimenter and the subject chased me down the hall, yelling, "Stop, wait a minute." They apologized and offered to explain what was really going on in the experiment.

They explained that typically approximately 65% of the teachers simply kept on shocking the individual—even after being told that the voltage increased for every error and that the student had a heart condition—as long as they were told that someone else took responsibility. They also told me that no shock was actually delivered (a second deception). The experiment was simply a test to see how far people would go if they were relieved of any responsibility for their actions. (They also told me that I would receive the two credits for the experiment even though my response was aberrant.)

The results of this experiment provided some insight into the behavior of Nazis and others during the Holocaust. The method, however, left a bad taste in my mouth and made me more cautious about taking part in any other psychology experiments. The experiment also shaped my behavior in the other experiments in which I did participate. I found myself routinely trying to figure out what reaction they were looking for—and then giving the opposite response. The researchers feared contaminating their study by sharing its purpose with me. As a result, I and probably many other students with similar responses deliberately contaminated several studies.

Ethnographers recognize this problem. They depend on the assistance of participants throughout their study. Such highly controlled, deceptive tactics are useful only for brief encounters. They are not useful in the long-term relationships that fieldwork requires. In addition, ethnographers are interested in how people think and behave in natural situations. Like any other researcher, anthropologists worry that participants are trying to tell them what they want to hear or are trying to second-guess the research agenda. Deceptive approaches reinforce this participant strategy and undermine the trust essential to any ethnographic effort.

Trust

Ethnographers need the trust of the people they work with to complete their task. An ethnographer who establishes a bond of trust will learn about the many layers of meaning in any community or program under study. Ethnographers build this bond on a foundation of honesty and communicate this trust verbally and nonverbally. They may speak simply and promise confidentiality as the need arises. Nonverbally, an ethnographer communicates this trust through self-presentation and general demeanor. Appropriate apparel, an open physical posture, handshakes, and other nonverbal cues can establish and maintain trust between an ethnographer and a participant.

Actions speak louder than words. An ethnographer's behavior in the field is usually the most effective means of cementing relationships and building trust. People like to talk, and ethnographers love to listen. As people learn that the ethnographer will respect and protect their conversations, they open up a little more each day in the belief that the researcher will not betray their trust. Trust can be an instant and spontaneous chemical reaction, but more often it is a long, steady process, like building a friendship.

Ethnographers usually maintain an implicit trust with the people they work with in a study. A powerful black leader invited me to his home to discuss his successful orchestration of political support for the dropout program. During the middle of this informal late-night interview, he explained why he would never hire a white person in his organization. He argued that the issue of qualifications was not pertinent and that hiring a white would rob a black of the job. Moreover, whites had made his life miserable, and hiring a white would be a form of "self-contempt and self-hatred."

This type of reverse discrimination did not become an issue at that time. The purpose of the meeting was to gain access to the leader's organization and to understand his worldview. He provided both in an extremely hospitable manner. The reverse discrimination discussion became relevant later in the study, however, as a guide to understanding the organizational dynamics of his institution. I collected the information without reaction because I had implicitly promised a nonjudgmental trust, and I never linked his name to the sentiment because he had spoken in confidence.

The demands of personal tolerance and trust came into play again when I was working as an assistant director and ethnographer in a senior citizen day care center. I was collecting initial interview data as a means of gaining the trust of program participants when I ran into Betsy. Betsy was a 90-year-old woman and one of the sweetest and friendliest individuals in the center. During my first lengthy conversation with her, she began rambling on, half in German and half in English. I tried a few timid questions in German about her youth, and she began to open up. During the conversation, I heard her repeat "Arbeit macht frei" (work makes you free) over and over again. In time, I realized she was referring to the legend inscribed over the entrances to concentration camps. My first impression was that she was a survivor, much like the survivors I had worked with in

Israel. I soon realized, however, that she was not a victim but a supporter of the Nazi movement. When I asked about the Jews and the Poles, she explained to me that "they deserved it" because they were the cause of her country's financial and moral bankruptcy. She had organized rallies for the Nazis and remembered one glorious moment when Adolf Hitler actually shook her hand. Betsy was my link to the women in the center. Everyone loved her, and she had befriended me. I had already extended an implicit trust. This ethical balancing act was one of the most difficult I have had to maintain as an ethnographer (Fetterman, 1986e).

People often accord ethnographers the same level of trust that they give to priests, rabbis, psychiatrists, clinical psychologists, doctors, and lawyers. The researcher must guard this trust, for better or worse, like a treasure. The ethnographer has an obligation to protect the privacy of his or her contacts. This obligation also protects the quality of the research effort. Errors, miscalculations, and poor judgment in human relations can be as devastating to the research effort as any notational or statistical error.

Pseudonyms

The project reaches maturity when the ethnographer has gained acceptance into the community or organization under study. Acceptance improves the quality of data by opening up new levels of previously undisclosed symbols and cultural knowledge. The issue of disclosing sacred cultural knowledge becomes more problematic after the ethnographer reaches this adult stage in the life cycle.

Ethnographic descriptions are usually detailed and revealing. They probe beyond the facade of normal human interaction. Such descriptions can jeopardize individuals. One person may speak candidly about a neighbor's wild parties and mention calling the police to complain about them. Another individual may reveal the arbitrary and punitive behavior of a program director or principal. Still another may simply reveal some information about office politics. Each individual has provided invaluable information about how the system really works. The delicate web of interrelationships in a neighborhood, a school, or an office, however, might be destroyed if the researcher reveals the source of this information. Similarly, individuals involved in illegal activity—ranging from handling venomous rattlesnakes in a religious ceremony to selling heroin in East Detroit to build a gang empire—have a legitimate concern about the repercussions of the researcher's disclosing their identity.

The use of pseudonyms is a simple way to disguise the identity of individuals and protect them from potential harm. Disguising the name of the village or program can also prevent the curious from descending on the community and disrupting the social fabric of its members' lives. Similarly, coding confidential data helps to prevent them from falling into the wrong hands.

In some instances, pseudonyms are not very helpful. Tribal villages have only one chief as a rule, schools have one principal, and social programs have one director. Pseudonyms, however, can still protect these individuals from the researcher's larger audience.

The ethnographer must exercise judgment in every instance in which an individual's identity becomes public. The ethnographer must decide whether the information is sufficiently important to justify effectively revealing the identity of the individual, whether the same information can be presented in another way or using other sources, or whether the finding must be abandoned because of the clear and present harm it represents to the participants. In addition, in many cases the culture or the program is public knowledge. In others, participants request that the researcher use their names (Booth, 1987). In these cases, ethnographers must use their judgment without being paternalistic.

Reciprocity

Ethnographers use a great deal of people's time, and they owe something in return. In some cases, ethnographers provide a service simply by lending a sympathetic ear to a troubled individual. In other situations, the ethnographer may offer time and expertise as barter—for example, teaching a participant English or math, milking cows and cleaning chicken coops, or helping a key actor set up a new computer and learn to use the software. Ethnographers also offer the results of their research in its final form as a type of reciprocity.

Some circumstances legitimate direct payment for services rendered, such as having participants help distribute questionnaires, hiring them as guides on expeditions, and soliciting various kinds of technical assistance. Direct payment, however, is not a highly recommended form of reciprocity. This approach often reinforces patterns of artificial dependence and fosters inappropriate expectations. Direct payment may also shape a person's responses or recommendations throughout a study. Reciprocity in some form is essential during fieldwork and, in some cases, after the study is complete, but it should not become an obtrusive, contaminating, or unethical activity.

Guilty Knowledge and Dirty Hands

During the more advanced stages of fieldwork, the ethnographer is likely to encounter the problems of guilty knowledge and dirty hands. *Guilty knowledge* is confidential knowledge of illegal or illicit activities. *Dirty hands* refers to situations in which the ethnographer cannot emerge innocent of wrongdoing (Fetterman, 1983; Klockars, 1977, 1979; Polsky, 1967).

During my study of the dropout program, I had established a bond of trust with the student who took me to the health food store to buy me a granola bar and show me his cultural knowledge of where to cop dope in the streets. I had confidential knowledge about illegal activities and was a participant—albeit a naive and unwilling one—in this activity. For me to turn in the student or the health food establishment in this case would have been unethical, however (Fetterman, 1983).

In another extremely sensitive situation, I judged it necessary to withhold potentially explosive information. While interviewing one of the students in an experimental program, I heard a scream. I left the student and ran to the source. The principal was already 20 feet ahead of me, pounding on the door, trying to force it open. The sounds emanating from the room by then were obviously sensual. When the principal forced the door open, we found one of the guidance counselors sexually engaged with a student. They had been upright against the door and were now half upright and half on the floor. The counselor was discreetly dismissed, and the student was temporarily dismissed and referred to an appropriate and responsible counseling center.

The principal and I spent the evening discussing the problem and our mutual responsibilities. I was convinced that this situation was atypical and that the principal had handled the matter appropriately. We knew that reporting this incident to the sponsors would permanently close the school down. As an ethnographer (and evaluator), I had ethical obligations to myriad individuals—ranging from the taxpayer to the students benefiting from the program and the more conscientious staff members. I eventually made my decision not to disclose the incident based on a traditional risk or cost-benefit analysis (Reynolds, 1979) and the recognition that reporting the incident would have represented methodological suicide (Fetterman, 1986e).

Rigorous Work

Ethics and quality are also intrinsic elements in ethnographic work. Ethnographers, like most scientists, work to produce a quality effort and product. Anything less represents an abdication of responsibility, diminishing the research effort and its credibility and impact.

Meeting scientific and ethical obligations to participants, colleagues, institutional sponsors, and taxpayers requires rigorous effort. Participants have the most at stake in any research endeavor: The information they provide can work for or against them. The ethnographer takes many precautions to protect the participant. The single most important guide to protecting participants is doing good work. An honest and thorough job presented in a clear and compelling manner will serve the participant well. A less than rigorous effort will result in misperceptions, misunderstandings, and factual inaccuracies that may confound the most altruistic parties in their efforts to understand and assist a group. Ethnographers must maintain the quality of the process as well as the outcome of their efforts. Producing a well-written description of a culture or group is not enough. The researcher must pursue each interview, observation, and analytical task with diligence. A lack of rigor or energy at any stage will diminish the quality and accuracy of the final product. Similarly, any decay in human relations during fieldwork will have an adverse impact on the ethnography or ethnographically informed report. Any of these weaknesses can endanger the group under study through misrepresentation and misunderstanding.

A rigorous effort contributes meaning to a knowledge base. A poorly designed or executed study only adds noise to the system, wasting time and energy that could have more productive use elsewhere. It also wastes the time of others who attempt to build on this shaky foundation. In addition, any activity that diminishes the credibility of scientific work through fraud or deception has a ripple effect; it tarnishes the reputation of the entire scientific community. Scientists without credibility cannot work effectively. Acts such as falsifying data, unprofessional behavior in the field, or plagiarism undermine faith in the integrity of the scholarly community (for a controversial case example of plagiarism in the field, see Fetterman, 1981a, 1981c; Rist, 1981).

Retirement and Last Rites

Retirement for the project comes at its completion—when the researcher has fulfilled the obligation to the sponsoring agency or has finished the study of a particular culture. The researcher's ethical obligation to the sponsor is to do the work the contract promises or at least to inform the sponsor of detours and possible alternate routes and directions. Last rites for the project come when the researcher is burned-out from the stress and is no longer producing high-quality work. Poor or unethical work may also bring on last rites by resulting in the withdrawal of funds, placing the participants (and the researcher) in a difficult position—particularly if the work is necessary to continued funding. It can also deprive peers of an opportunity to use the same funds in a more productive and professional manner.

Lack of rigor can also place the sponsor in jeopardy. The sponsor is accountable to various parties—for example, most federal sponsors are answerable to Congress. Sponsors who demonstrate a poor track record in selecting researchers or producing research information for a specific policy decision may not have another opportunity to do so in the future. Their jobs, as well as the jobs of those they may have assisted with well-executed research, are at risk. Government sponsors have an ultimate responsibility to the taxpayer to solve basic social problems. Abrogations in any of these areas are cues for the ethnographer to consider retiring from the project or from the discipline.

Ethics guide the first and last steps of an ethnography. Ethnographers stand at ethical crossroads throughout their research. This fact of ethnographic life sharpens the senses and ultimately refines and enhances the quality of the endeavor.

CONCLUSION

Ethnographers must wander through a multicultural wilderness, learning to see the world through the eyes of people from all walks of life. The ethnographic journey takes the researcher on paths that lead nowhere, past tempting hazards and deceptively open marshes. Without sufficient preparation, this journey can become nightmarish.

Before beginning their travels through an unfamiliar culture, ethnographers must be able to identify and select appropriate problems and must learn to use theory, concepts, methods, techniques, and appropriate equipment in the field. Ethnographers must also be able to analyze their data and write about what they observe and record in an articulate and cogent manner. In addition, they must learn how to manage the multitude of ethical dilemmas they face at every turn.

This book aims to guide novice ethnographers through the cultural wilds they must negotiate. Each chapter provides a landmark along the trail. The irony is that good ethnography requires the researcher to pursue the detours as well as the paths and to become lost in the culture to learn its terrain. I hope that this book will be a useful guide for the initiate, a tool for the teacher, and a refresher for the experienced ethnographer. Those who find themselves just beginning the journey and a little overwhelmed by the distance yet to travel may find some comfort in the sage advice of Lao-tzu: "A journey of a thousand miles must begin with a single step."

References

Agar, M. (1980). *The professional stranger.* New York: Academic Press.

Agar, M. (1986). *Speaking of ethnography.* Beverly Hills, CA: Sage.

Bank, A. (1986). [Review of the book *Ethnography in educational evaluation*]. *Evaluation and Program Planning, 9,* 180-183.

Barnett, H. G. (1953). *Innovation: The basis of culture change.* New York: McGraw-Hill.

Barzun, J. (1984). *Simple & direct: A rhetoric for writers* (Rev. ed.). New York: Harper & Row.

Basham, R., & DeGroot, D. (1977). Current approaches to the anthropology of urban and complex societies. *American Anthropologist, 79,* 414-440.

Becker, H. S. (1979). Do photographs tell the truth? In T. D. Cook & C. S. Reichardt (Eds.), *Qualitative and quantitative methods in evaluation research.* Beverly Hills, CA: Sage.

Bee, R. L. (1974). *Patterns and processes: An introduction to anthropological strategies for the study of sociocultural change.* New York: Free Press.

Bellman, B. L., & Jules-Rosette, B. (1977). *A paradigm for looking: Cross-cultural research with visual media.* Norwood, NJ: Ablex.

Bernstein, T. M. (1965). *The careful writer: A modern guide to English usage.* New York: Atheneum.

Bernstein, T. M. (1977). *Dos, don'ts, & maybes of English usage.* New York: Times Books.

Birdwhistell, R. L. (1970). *Kinesics and context: Essays on body motion communication.* Philadelphia: University of Pennsylvania Press.

Blalock, H. M. (1979). *Social statistics.* New York: McGraw-Hill.

Blumer, H. (1969). *Symbolic interactionism: Perspective and method.* Englewood Cliffs, NJ: Prentice Hall.

Bogdan, R. C., & Biklen, S. K. (1982). *Qualitative research for education: An introduction to theory and methods.* Boston: Allyn & Bacon.

Bogdan, R. C., & Taylor, S. J. (1975). *Introduction to qualitative research methods: A phenomenological approach to the social sciences.* New York: John Wiley.

Bohannan, P., & Middleton, J. (1968). *Kinship and social organization.* New York: Natural History Press.

Bonk, C. J., Appleman, R., & Hay, K. E. (1996, Sept./Oct.). Electronic conferencing tools for student apprenticeship and perspective taking. *Educational Technology,* pp. 8-18.

Booth, E. O. (1987). Researcher as participant: Collaborative evaluation in a primary school. In D. M. Fetterman (Ed.), Perennial issues in qualitative research [Special issue]. *Education and Urban Society, 20*(1), 55-85.

Brent, E. (1984). Qualitative computing approaches and issues. *Qualitative Sociology, 7,* 61-74.

148   ETHNOGRAPHY

Brim, J. A., & Spain, D. H. (1974). *Research design in anthropology: Paradigms and pragmatics in the testing of hypotheses.* New York: Holt, Rinehart & Winston.

Britan, G. M. (1978). Experimental and contextual models of program evaluation. *Evaluation and Program Planning, 1,* 229-234.

Burbules, N. C., & Bruce, B. C. (1995). This is not a paper. *Educational Researcher, 24*(8), 12-18.

Burnett, J. H. (1976). Ceremony, rites, and economy in the student system of an American high school. In J. I. Roberts & S. K. Akinsanya (Eds.), *Educational patterns and cultural configurations* (pp. 313-323). New York: David McKay.

Cazden, C. B. (1979). *Peekaboo as an instructional strategy: Discourse development at home and at school* (Papers and Reports on Child Language Development, No. 17). Stanford, CA: Stanford University, Department of Linguistics.

Chagnon, N. A. (1977). *Yanomamo: The fierce people.* New York: Holt, Rinehart & Winston.

Claremont, L. de (1938). *Legends of incense, herb and oil magic.* Dallas: Dorene.

Collier, J. (1967). *Visual anthropology: Photography as a research method.* New York: Holt, Rinehart & Winston.

Computer-assisted anthropology [Special section]. (1984). *Practicing Anthropology, 6*(2), 1-17.

Conrad, P., & Reinharz, S. (1984). Computers and qualitative data. *Qualitative Sociology, 7,* 1-2.

Cook, T. D., & Campbell, D. T. (1979). *Quasi-experimentation: Design and analysis issues for field settings.* Chicago: Rand McNally.

Daner, F. J. (1976). *The American children of Krisna: A study of the Hare Krisna movement.* New York: Holt, Rinehart & Winston.

Deng, F. M. (1972). *The Dinka of the Sudan.* New York: Holt, Rinehart & Winston. (Reissued by Waveland Press)

Denzin, N. K. (1978). *The research act: A theoretical introduction to sociological methods.* New York: McGraw-Hill.

Dobbert, M. L. (1982). *Ethnographic research: Theory and application for modern schools and societies.* New York: Praeger.

Dolgin, J. L., Kemnitzer, D. S., & Schneider, D. M. (1977). *Symbolic anthropology: A reader in the study of symbols and meanings.* New York: Columbia University Press.

Dorr-Bremme, D. W. (1985). Ethnographic evaluation: A theory and method. *Educational Evaluation and Policy Analysis, 7*(1), 65-83.

Downs, J. F. (1972). *The Navajo.* New York: Holt, Rinehart & Winston. (Reissued by Waveland Press)

Ellen, R. F. (1984). *Ethnographic research: A guide to general conduct.* New York: Academic Press.

Erickson, F. (1976). Gatekeeping encounters: A social selection process. In P. R. Sanday (Ed.), *Anthropology and the public interest: Fieldwork and theory.* New York: Academic Press.

Erickson, F., & Wilson, J. (1982). *Sights and sounds of life in schools: A resource guide to film and videotape for research and education.* East Lansing: Michigan State University, Institute for Research on Teaching of the College of Education.

Evans-Pritchard, E. E. (1940). *The Nuer: A description of the modes of livelihood and political institutions of a nilotic people.* New York: Oxford University Press.

Evans-Pritchard, E. E. (1951). *Social anthropology.* London: Cohen & West.

Fetterman, D. M. (1980). Ethnographic techniques in educational evaluation: An illustration. In A. Van Fleet (Ed.), Anthropology of education: Methods and applications [Special issue]. *Journal of Thought, 15*(3), 31-48.

Fetterman, D. M. (1981a). A new peril for the contract ethnographer. *Anthropology and Education Quarterly, 12*(1), 71-80.

Fetterman, D. M. (1981b). Blaming the victim: The problem of evaluation design and federal involvement, and reinforcing world views in education. *Human Organization, 40*(1), 67-77.

Fetterman, D. M. (1981c). Protocol and publication: Ethical obligations. *Anthropology and Education Quarterly, 12*(1), 82-83.

Fetterman, D. M. (1982a). Ethnography in educational research: The dynamics of diffusion. *Educational Researcher, 11*(3), 17-29.

Fetterman, D. M. (1982b). Ibsen's baths: Reactivity and insensitivity—A misapplication of the treatment-control design in a national evaluation. *Educational Evaluation and Policy Analysis, 4*(3), 261-279.

Fetterman, D. M. (1983). Guilty knowledge, dirty hands, and other ethical dilemmas: The hazards of contract research. *Human Organization, 42*(3), 214-224.

Fetterman, D. M. (1984). *Ethnography in educational evaluation.* Beverly Hills, CA: Sage.

Fetterman, D. M. (1986a). A response to Adrianne Bank: The role of informed criticism in scholarly review. *Evaluation and Program Planning, 9,* 183-184.

Fetterman, D. M. (1986b). Beyond the status quo in ethnographic educational evaluation. In D. M. Fetterman & M. A. Pitman (Eds.), *Educational evaluation: Ethnography in theory, practice, and politics.* Beverly Hills, CA: Sage.

Fetterman, D. M. (1986c). {Review of the book *Ethnography and qualitative design in educational research*]. *American Anthropologist, 88*(3), 764-765.

Fetterman, D. M. (1986d). [Review of the book *The politics of education: Culture, power, and liberation*]. *American Anthropologist, 88*(1), 253-254.

Fetterman, D. M. (1986e). Conceptual crossroads: Methods and ethics in ethnographic evaluation. In D. D. Williams (Ed.), *Naturalistic evaluation* (New Directions for Program Evaluation 30). San Francisco: Jossey-Bass.

Fetterman, D. M. (1986f). Gifted and talented education: A national test case in Peoria. *Educational Evaluation and Policy Analysis, 8*(2), 155-166.

Fetterman, D. M. (1986g). Operational auditing: A cultural approach. *Internal Auditor, 43*(2), 48-54.

Fetterman, D. M. (1987a). Ethnographic educational evaluation. In G. D. Spindler (Ed.), *Interpretive ethnography of education: At home and abroad.* Hillsdale, NJ: Lawrence Erlbaum.

Fetterman, D. M. (1987b, November 18-22). *Multiple audiences reflect multiple realities.* Invited presentation at the 86th Annual Meeting of the American Anthropological Association, Chicago.

Fetterman, D. M. (1988a). *Excellence and equality: A qualitatively different perspective on gifted and talented education.* Albany: State University of New York Press.

Fetterman, D. M. (1988b). *Qualitative approaches to evaluation in education: The silent scientific revolution.* New York: Praeger.

Fetterman, D. M. (1996a). Ethnography in the virtual classroom. *Practicing Anthropology, 18*(3), 2, 36-39.

Fetterman, D. M. (1996b). Videoconferencing on-line: Enhancing communication over the Internet. *Educational Researcher, 25*(4), 23-27.

Fetterman, D. M. (1996c, June). [Book review]. *American Anthropologist, 98*(2), 16-17.

Fetterman, D. M., Kaftarian, S. J., & Wandersman, A. (1996). *Empowerment evaluation: Knowledge and tools for self-assessment and accountability.* Thousand Oaks, CA: Sage.

Fetterman, D. M., & Pitman, M. A. (Eds.). (1986). *Educational evaluation: Ethnography in theory, practice, and politics.* Beverly Hills, CA: Sage.

Fischer, M. D. (1994). *Applications in computing for social anthropologists.* London: Routledge.

Fletcher, C. (1970). *The complete walker: The joys and techniques of hiking and backpacking.* New York: Knopf.

Fowler, F. J. (1988). *Survey research methods* (Rev. ed.). Newbury Park, CA: Sage.

Freilick, M. (Ed.). (1970). *Marginal natives: Anthropologists at work.* New York: Harper & Row.

Gamache, H. (1942). *The master book of candle burning or how to burn candles for every purpose.* Highland Falls, NY: Sheldon.

Garfinkel, H. (1967). *Studies in ethnomethodology.* Englewood Cliffs, NJ: Prentice Hall.

Geertz, C. (1957). Ritual and social change: A Javanese example. *American Anthropologist, 59,* 32-54.

Geertz, C. (1963). *Agricultural involution.* Berkeley: University of California Press.

Geertz, C. (1973). *The interpretation of cultures.* New York: Basic Books.

Glaser, B., & Strauss, A. L. (1967). *The discovery of grounded theory: Strategies for qualitative research.* Chicago: Aldine.

Glass, S. (1997, January 6). Markets and myths: Autonomy in public and private schools. *Education Policy Analysis Archives, 5*(1).

Gluckman, M. (1968). The utility of the equilibrium model in the study of social change. *American Anthropologist, 70*(2), 219-237.

Goetz, J. P., & LeCompte, M. D. (1984). *Ethnography and qualitative design in educational research.* New York: Academic Press.

Groves, R. M., & Kahn, R. L. (1979). *Surveys by telephone: A national comparison with personal interviews.* New York: Academic Press.

Gumperz, J. (1972). The speech community. In P. P. Giglioli (Ed.), *Language and social context.* Harmondsworth, UK: Penguin.

Guttman, L. (1944). A basis for scaling qualitative data. *American Sociological Review, 9,* 139-150.

Habermas, J. (1968). *Knowledge and human interests.* Boston: Beacon.

Hagburg, E. (1970). Validity of questionnaire data: Reported and observed attendance in an adult education program. In D. P. Forcese & S. Richer (Eds.), *Stages of social research: Contemporary perspectives.* Englewood Cliffs, NJ: Prentice Hall.

Hall, E. T. (1974). *Handbook for proxemic research.* Washington, DC: Society for the Anthropology of Visual Communication.

Hammersley, M., & Atkinson, P. (1983). *Ethnography: Principles in practice.* New York: Tavistock.

Harris, M. (1968). *The rise of anthropological theory.* New York: Thomas Y. Crowell.

Harris, M. (1971). *Culture, man, and nature.* New York: Thomas Y. Crowell.

Hart, C. W. M., & Pilling, A. R. (1960). *The Tiwi of North Australia.* New York: Holt, Rinehart & Winston.

Heath, S. B. (1982). Questions at home and school. In G. Spindler (Ed.), *Doing the ethnography of schooling: Educational anthropology in action.* New York: Holt, Rinehart & Winston.

Heider, K. G. (1976). *Ethnographic film*. Austin: University of Texas Press.

Hockings, P. (Ed.). (1975). *Principles of visual anthropology*. The Hague: Mouton.

Hopkins, K. D., & Glass, G. V (1978). *Basic statistics for the behavioral sciences*. Englewood Cliffs, NJ: Prentice Hall.

Hopkins, K. D., Hopkins, B. R., & Glass, G. V. (1996). *Basic statistics for the behavioral sciences* (3rd ed.). Boston: Allyn & Bacon.

Hostetler, J. A., & Huntington, G. E. (1967). *The Hutterites in North America*. New York: Holt, Rinehart & Winston.

Hostetler, J. A., & Huntington, G. E. (1971). *Children in Amish society: Socializing and community education*. New York: Holt, Rinehart & Winston.

Jacobs, J. (1974). *Fun city: An ethnographic study of a retirement community*. New York: Holt, Rinehart & Winston. (Reissued by Waveland Press)

Jacoby, R. (1987). *The last intellectuals: American culture in the age of academe*. New York: Basic Books.

Janesick, V. J. (1986). [Review of the book *Ethnography in educational evaluation*]. *American Journal of Education*, 555-558.

Kaplan, D., & Manners, R. A. (1972). *Culture theory*. Englewood Cliffs, NJ: Prentice Hall. (Reissued by Waveland Press)

Keiser, R. L. (1969). *The vice lords: Warriors of the street*. New York: Holt, Rinehart & Winston.

King, A. R. (1967). *The school at Mopass: A problem of identity*. New York: Holt, Rinehart & Winston.

Klockars, C. B. (1977). Field ethics for the life history. In R. S. Weppner (Ed.), *Street ethnography: Selected studies of crime and drug use in natural settings*. Beverly Hills, CA: Sage.

Klockars, C. B. (1979). Dirty hands and deviant subjects. In C. B. Klockars & F. W. O'Connor (Eds.), *Deviance and decency: The ethics of research with human subjects*. Beverly Hills, CA: Sage.

Lareau, A. (1987). Teaching qualitative methods: The role of classroom activities. In D. M. Fetterman (Ed.), Perennial issues in qualitative research [Special issue]. *Education and Urban Society, 20*(1), 86-120.

Lavrakas, P. J. (1987). *Telephone survey methods*. Newbury Park, CA: Sage.

Levine, H. G. (1985). Principles of data storage and retrieval for use in qualitative evaluations. *Educational Evaluation and Policy Analysis, 7*(2), 169-186.

Maxwell, J. A., Bashook, P. G., & Sandlow, L. J. (1986). Combining ethnographic and experimental methods in educational evaluation: A case study. In D. M. Fetterman & M. A. Pitman (Eds.), *Educational evaluation: Ethnography in theory, practice, and politics*. Beverly Hills, CA: Sage.

McDermott, R. P. (1974). Achieving school failure: An anthropological approach to illiteracy and social stratification. In G. D. Spindler (Ed.), *Education and cultural process: Toward an anthropology of education*. New York: Holt, Rinehart & Winston.

McFee, M. (1972). *Modern Blackfeet: Montanans on a reservation*. New York: Holt, Rinehart & Winston. (Reissued by Waveland Press)

Mehan, H. (1987). Language and schooling. In G. D. Spindler (Ed.), *Interpretive ethnography of education: At home and abroad*. Hillsdale, NJ: Lawrence Erlbaum.

Mehan, H., & Wood, H. (1975). *The reality of ethnomethodology*. New York: John Wiley.

Miles, M. B., & Huberman, A. M. (1984). *Qualitative data analysis: A sourcebook of new methods*. Beverly Hills, CA: Sage.

Mills, C. (1959). *The sociological imagination*. New York: Oxford University Press.

Ogbu, J. U. (1978). *Minority education and caste: The American system in cross-cultural perspective.* New York: Academic Press.

Osgood, C. (1964). Semantic differential technique in the comparative study of cultures. In A. K. Romney & R. G. D'Andrade (Eds.), Transcultural studies in cognition [Special issue]. *American Anthropologist, 66.*

Patton, M. Q. (1980). *Qualitative evaluation methods.* Beverly Hills, CA: Sage.

Pelto, P. J. (1970). *Anthropological research: The structure of inquiry.* New York: Harper & Row.

Pelto, P. J., & Pelto, G. H. (1978). *Anthropological research: The structure of inquiry* (2nd ed.). Cambridge, UK: Cambridge University Press.

Phelan, P. (1987). Compatibility of qualitative and quantitative methods: Studying child sexual abuse in America. In D. M. Fetterman (Ed.), Perennial issues in qualitative research [Special issue]. *Education and Urban Society, 20*(1), 35-41.

Pi-Sunyer, O., & Salzmann, Z. (1978). *Humanity and culture: An introduction to anthropology.* Boston: Houghton Mifflin.

Pitman, M. A., & Dobbert, M. L. (1986). The use of explicit anthropological theory in educational evaluation: A case study. In D. M. Fetterman & M. A. Pitman (Eds.), *Educational evaluation: Ethnography in theory, practice, and politics.* Beverly Hills, CA: Sage.

Podolefsky, A., & McCarthy, C. (1983). Topical sorting: A technique for computer assisted qualitative data analysis. *American Anthropologist, 85,* 886-890.

Polsky, N. (1967). *Hustlers, beats, and others.* Chicago: Aldine.

Powdermaker, H. (1966). *Stranger and friend: The way of an anthropologist.* New York: Norton.

Powell, W. W. (1985). *Getting into print: The decision-making process in scholarly publishing.* Chicago: University of Chicago Press.

Radcliffe-Brown, A. R. (1952). *Structure and function in primitive society.* New York: Free Press.

Reynolds, P. D. (1979). *Ethical dilemmas and social science research.* San Francisco: Jossey-Bass.

Rist, R. (1981). Shadow versus substance: A reply to David Fetterman. *Anthropology and Education Quarterly, 12*(1), 81-82.

Rosenfeld, G. (1971). *"Shut those thick lips!": A study of slum school failure.* New York: Holt, Rinehart & Winston. (Reissued by Waveland Press)

Rynkiewich, M. A., & Spradley, J. P. (1976). *Ethics and anthropology: Dilemmas in fieldwork.* New York: John Wiley.

Schwandt, T. A., & Halpern, E. S. (1988). *Linking auditing and meta-evaluation.* Newbury Park, CA: Sage.

Schwimmer, B. (1996). Review and evaluation of anthropology on the Internet. *Current Anthropology, 37*(3), 561.

Shavelson, R. J. (1996). *Statistical reasoning for the behavioral sciences* (3rd ed.). Boston: Allyn & Bacon.

Shultz, J., & Florio, S. (1979). Stop and freeze: The negotiation of social and physical space in a kindergarten/first grade classroom. *Anthropology and Education Quarterly, 10,* 166-181.

Simon, E. L. (1986). Theory in educational evaluation: Or, what's wrong with generic-brand anthropology. In D. M. Fetterman & M. A. Pitman (Eds.), *Educational evaluation: Ethnography in theory, practice, and politics.* Beverly Hills, CA: Sage.

Society for the Anthropology of Visual Communication. *Studies in the anthropology of visual communication.* Philadelphia: Annenberg School Press.

Spindler, G. (1955). *Sociocultural and psychological processes in Menomini acculturation* (Publications in Culture and Society, No. 5). Berkeley: University of California Press.

Spindler, G., & Goldschmidt, W. R. (1952). Experimental design in the study of culture change. *Southwestern Journal of Anthropology, 8,* 68-83.

Spindler, G. D., & Spindler, L. (1958). Male and female adaptations in culture change. *American Anthropologist, 60,* 217-233.

Spindler, G. D., & Spindler, L. (1970). *Being an anthropologist: Fieldwork in eleven cultures.* New York: Holt, Rinehart & Winston. (Reissued by Waveland Press)

Spindler, L. (1962). Menomini women and culture change. *American Anthropological Association Memoir, 91.*

Spradley, J. P. (1970). *You owe yourself a drunk: An ethnography of urban nomads.* Boston: Little, Brown.

Spradley, J. P. (1979). *The ethnographic interview.* New York: Holt, Rinehart & Winston.

Spradley, J. P. (1980). *Participant observation.* New York: Holt, Rinehart & Winston.

Spradley, J. P., & McCurdy, D. W. (1972). *The cultural experience: Ethnography in complex society.* Palo Alto, CA: Science Research Associates.

Spradley, J. P., & McCurdy, D. W. (1975). *Anthropology: The cultural perspective.* New York: John Wiley.

Sproull, L. S., & Sproull, R. F. (1982). Managing and analyzing behavior records: Explorations in nonnumeric data analysis. *Human Organization, 41,* 283-290.

Strunk, W., & White, E. B. (1959). *The elements of style.* Toronto: Macmillan.

Studstill, J. D. (1986). Attribution in Zairian secondary schools: Ethnographic evaluation and sociocultural systems. In D. M. Fetterman & M. A. Pitman (Eds.), *Educational evaluation: Ethnography in theory, practice, and politics.* Beverly Hills, CA: Sage.

Tax, S. (1958). The Fox project. *Human Organization, 17,* 17-19.

Taylor, S. J., & Bogdan, R. (1984). *Introduction to qualitative research methods: The search for meanings.* New York: John Wiley.

Tonkinson, R. (1974). *The Jigalong Mob: Aboriginal victors of the desert crusade.* Menlo Park, CA: Cummings.

Van Til, W. (1987). *Writing for professional publication.* Newton, MA: Allyn & Bacon.

Vogt, E. (1960). On the concepts of structure and process in cultural anthropology. *American Anthropologist, 62*(1), 18-33.

Weaver, T. (1973). *To see ourselves: Anthropology and modern social issues.* Glenview, IL: Scott, Foresman.

Webb, E. J., Campbell, D. T., Schwartz, R. D., & Sechrest, L. (1966). *Unobtrusive measures: Nonreactive research in the social sciences.* Chicago: Rand McNally.

Weitzman, E. A., & Miles, M. B. (1995). *Computer programs for qualitative data analysis: A software sourcebook.* Thousand Oaks, CA: Sage.

Werner, O., & Schoepfle, G. M. (1987a). *Systematic fieldwork* (Vol. 1). Newbury Park, CA: Sage.

Werner, O., & Schoepfle, G. M. (1987b). *Systematic fieldwork* (Vol. 2). Newbury Park, CA: Sage.

Whyte, W. F. (1955). *Street corner society: The social structure of an Italian slum.* Chicago: University of Chicago Press.

Wolcott, H. F. (1973). *The man in the principal's office: An ethnography.* New York: Holt, Rinehart & Winston. (Reissued by Waveland Press)

Wolcott, H. F. (1975). Criteria for an ethnographic approach to research in schools. *Human Organization, 34,* 111-127.

Wolcott, H. F. (1980). How to look like an anthropologist without really being one. *Practicing Anthropology, 3*(2), 39.

Wolcott, H. F. (1982). Mirrors, models, and monitors: Educator adaptations of the ethnographic innovation. In G. D. Spindler (Ed.), *Doing the ethnography of schooling: Educational anthropology in action.* New York: Holt, Rinehart & Winston.

Wolf, A. (1970). Childhood association and sexual attraction: A further test of the Westermarck hypothesis. *American Anthropologist, 72,* 503-515.

Yin, R. K. (1984). *Case study research: Design and methods.* Beverly Hills, CA: Sage.

Name Index

Subject Index

Jews, 142
  Hasidic, 36
Joint Dissemination Review Panel
  Submission, 135

Krsna, 29

Leaving the field, 10
Library of Congress, 62, 74, 87
Library studies, 8-9, 34, 41-43, 61-62, 101
Life histories, 9

Man in the Principal's Office, The, 28
Manhattan, 65
Methods, 13, 31-62
  entry, 33-34
    intermediary, 33-34
  fieldwork, 1, 8, 9, 31-32, 35-37
  folktales, 60-61
  interviewing, 37-52
    expressive autobiographical
      interviews, 51-52
    informal interviews, 38-40
    interviewing protocols, 44-47
    key actor or informant interviewing,
      47-51
    life histories, 51-52
    open-ended or closed-ended
      questions, 43-44
    privacy, 40
    rapport, 38, 46, 64, 79
    retrospective, 40
    silence, 47
    specific questions, 42-43
      attribute questions, 42-43, 62
      structural questions, 42-43
    survey or grand tour question, 40-42
    structured and semistructured
      interviews, 38
  participant observation, 34-37
  nonparticipant observation, 37
  projective techniques, 55-56, 65
    Rorschach ink blot tests, 55
    Thematic Apperception Test, 55
  questionnaires, 53-55
    Likert-type scale, 57

selection and sampling, 8, 32-33, 106
  criterian-based, 33
  judgmental sampling, 8, 33, 106
  probabilistic, 33
  randomized, 33, 106
triangulation, 2, 9, 46, 69
unobtrusive measures, 57-61
  kinesics, 59-60
  outcroppings, 49, 57
  proxemics, 59-60
  written and electronic
    information, 58-59
Michigan, 80
Milgram study, 139-140
Multicultural, 5
Multiple Realities, 6, 20, 21

Navajo, 29
Nazi, 26, 51, 140
  Arbeit Macht Frei, 141
  concentration camps, 141
  survivors, 51, 141
New York, 65
Nonjudgmental orientation, 2

Patterns, 17, 68, 77, 96-98
Phenomenology, 5, 20, 22
Physicians, 21
Planning, 2, 9
Poles, 142
Positivism, 5, 22
Powerbook, 72, 73
Practicing Anthropology, 84
Problem identification, 1, 2, 3
Process, 105
Proposal, 8

Quasi-experimental design, 3

Reliability, 33, 36, 76, 96-98
  patterns, 17
Research Design, 1-2, 3, 8-10
Research Laboratory study, 94-95,
  108-109
Research Life Cycle, 136-146

About the Author

David M. Fetterman is Professor, Director of the Policy Analysis and Evaluation master's degree program at Stanford University, and a member of the faculty at Sierra Nevada College. He was formerly professor and research director at the California Institute of Integral Studies;

 principal research scientist at the American Institutes for Research; and a senior associate and project director at RMC Research Corporation. He received his Ph.D. from Stanford University in educational and medical anthropology. He has conducted fieldwork in both Israel (including living on a kibbutz) and the United States (primarily in inner cities throughout the country). He works in the fields of educational evaluation, ethnography, and policy analysis and focuses on programs for dropouts and gifted and talented education. He is a past president of the American Evaluation Association and the American Anthropological Association's Council on Anthropology and Education.

He has also served as the program chair for both of these organizations. He has conducted extensive multisite evaluation research on local, state, and national levels. His multisite work has been primarily in urban settings. He conducted a 3-year national evaluation of dropout programs for the Department of Education. In addition, he served as the director of an antipoverty program. He has also conducted research on migrant and bilingual education programs. David has taught in an inner-city high school, in two Hebrew schools, and in various university settings.

Although he is recognized for his contributions to the development of ethnographic evaluation, his recent efforts have focused on developing empowerment evaluation—to help people help themselves. He has used this approach throughout the United States and in South Africa. David has been elected a fellow of the American Anthropological Association and the Society for Applied Anthropology. He received the Myrdal Award for Evaluation Practice—the American Evaluation Association's highest honor. He also received the George and Louise Spindler Award for outstanding contributions to educational anthropology as a scholar and practitioner and the Ethnographic Evaluation Award from the Council on Anthropology and Education. He received the President's Award from the Evaluation Research Society for contributions to ethnographic educational evaluation. He was also awarded the Washington Association of Practicing Anthropologists' Praxis Publication Award for translating knowledge into action.

David has also worked on the state, national, and international levels in the field of gifted and talented education. He created and organized the first and second Gifted and Talented Education Conference at Stanford University. He received one of the 1990 Mensa Education and Research Foundation Awards for Excellence. Mensa Education and Research Foundation encourages research into the nature, characteristics, and uses of intelligence. The award was made for his book, *Excellence and Equality: A Qualitatively Different Perspective on Gifted and Talented Education,* and for articles on gifted and talented education in *Educational Evaluation and Policy Analysis* and *Gifted Education International.* David was appointed by the U.S. Department of Education to serve on a panel to select a national center for the gifted and talented. He was selected in part because of his recommendation to create a national center in his book *Excellence and Equality.* The center is currently operating, and he is a member of the center's Consultant Bank, currently advising the National Research Center on the Gifted and Talented. David has taught on-line on the Internet for more than 4 years in an on-line Ph.D. program. He also uses virtual classrooms at Stanford University to complement face-to-face instruction. He writes about teaching on-line and videoconferencing on the Internet in many journals, including *Educational Researcher* and *Practicing Anthropology.* He maintains an American Evaluation Association division listserv for collaborative, participatory, and empowerment evaluation. David was recently appointed to the American Educational Research

Association's Telecommunications Committee and advises the association in this area. He has consulted for a variety of federal agencies, foundations, corporations, and academic institutions, including the U.S. Department of Education, National Institute of Mental Health, Centers for Disease Control, W. K. Kellogg Foundation, Rockefeller Foundation, Walter S. Johnson Foundation, Syntex, the Independent Development Trust in South Africa, Early Childhood Research Institute on Full Inclusion, and universities throughout the United States and Europe.

David is the general editor for Garland/Taylor and Francis Publication's *Studies in Education and Culture* series. He has contributed to a variety of encyclopedias, including the *International Encyclopedia of Education* and *The Encyclopedia of Human Intelligence.* He is also author of *Empowerment Evaluation: Knowledge and Tools for Self-Assessment and Accountability; Speaking the Language of Power: Communication, Collaboration, and Advocacy; Ethnography: Step by Step; Qualitative Approaches to Evaluation in Education: The Silent Scientific Revolution; Excellence and Equality: A Qualitatively Different Perspective on Gifted and Talented Education; Educational Evaluation: Ethnography in Theory, Practice, and Politics*; and *Ethnography in Educational Evaluation.*

APPLIED SOCIAL RESEARCH
METHODS SERIES

Series Editors
LEONARD BICKMAN, Peabody College, Vanderbilt University, Nashville
DEBRA J. ROG, Vanderbilt University, Washington, DC

Other volumes in this series are listed on the series page